CREDIT-CARDSMANSHIP:

How to Survive the Credit Card Nightmare and Turn Plastic Into Gold

By Martin J. Meyer

Farnsworth Publishing Company, Inc.
Lynbrook, New York • 1971

CREDIT-CARDSMANSHIP

Table of Contents

PART THREE:

HIDDEN DANGERS IN YOUR PLASTICS:
THEY COULD RUIN YOUR LIFE

PART FOUR:

THE PLASTICS SOCIETY:
IT CAN MOLD YOUR LIFE TODAY,
AND TURN IT INTO A NIGHTMARE TOMORROW

PART ONE

HIDDEN ADVANTAGES IN YOUR PLASTIC: YOU CAN TURN THEM INTO GOLD

CHAPTER I

Making Money and Saving Money With Your Credit Cards: The Rules of the Game

---

There are "hidden" advantages to the credit card that can swell your bank account, while you enjoy the luxuries of our affluent society. There are "hidden" disadvantages that can push you over the brink of bankruptcy, and threaten your privacy and even your freedom and individuality. The credit card game is played for high stakes. Here are the basic rules which you must know in order to play the game—to win.

With credit cards, you can:
- —earn at a rate of more than 7 percent, on money you've already spent
- —get the cash you need when you need it, even when the banks refuse you a loan
- —slash the cost of credit on your own credit cards, by as much as 33⅓ percent
- —obtain discounts of 7 percent and more, even on close-out sales
- —use substantial sums of money for as long as three months, at no cost to you
- —pay for things more cheaply than with traveler's checks, or even free checks
- —obtain virtually unlimited credit, on an average income

1

—raise thousands of dollars in cash on a credit ceiling of $500 or less, with no approval necessary.

These advantages are built into the credit card system. They're "hidden" advantages, and never publicized. They're brought to light in this book.

*   *   *

Also exposed are the loopholes in the credit card system which enable sharp operators to "take" credit card services for sizeable sums of money, and stay, perhaps, within the law. With credit cards, these operators can:
— wipe out old debts without paying them, and start life anew with $30,000 or more, with no strings attached
— take a trip around the world, live luxuriously for months without working, throw lavish parties, shower friends and relatives with expensive gifts, and never pay the bills
— earn up to 155 percent per year on bank "loans" that the bank never knew it made, and pay no interest or any other charges
— raise the big money for that one big chance on the horses, the stock market, the get-rich-quick proposition, and, in case of loss, never have to pay back a cent.

*   *   *

Little known, too, are many of the dangers of the credit card. "Invisible changes are taking place . . . and they are . . . cataclysmic," Ralph Nader explains. "There is abysmal ignorance on the subject because the stakes are very high [to the people who control the credit card system] in terms of ignoring the whole question." That question—the "hidden" hazards of the credit card—is explored in this book in detail. Because of the credit card, you can be:

—robbed of thousands of dollars, and not even know it
until the credit card services present the bills
—seduced onto a treadmill of unmanageable debt for
the rest of your life
—forced to pay higher prices on everything you buy
because of the "hidden costs" of the credit card, even
when you buy for cash
—victimized by computer errors which can cost you
thousands of dollars, and ruin your credit standing
and reputation
—threatened with the loss of your savings as credit card
financing weakens the banking structure and makes
it difficult for the Federal deposit insurance agencies
to protect you against bank failures
—stripped of your privacy by credit investigators who
know how much you drink, why you were divorced,
what political meetings you attend—and who store
up all the information in computers which make your
life's history available to anybody at the touch of a
button.

And worse: In the world that the credit card is now
spawning, you could lose your freedom. In that world, there'll
be only one way to buy anything—the credit card way. You'll
only be able to live by using your credit card, and you'll
only be able to use your credit card if the computer approves,
and the computer will approve only if the people who control
the computer approve. "This is leading to a significant kind
of tyranny," Ralph Nader warns. "The key democratic principle of a man's control over his life is being abused. And unless we do something about it, we're suddenly going to wake
up and realize we're a nation of slaves."

*   *   *

The credit card, then, is far from a simple device for
buying now and paying later. Using the credit card is like

playing a complex game for high stakes: For big money and for your own well-being, security and dignity. Win—and you can enjoy the goods and services of the most affluent society the world has ever seen—at bargain rates—and make extra money while you're doing it. Lose—and you could be taken to the cleaners, stand by helplessly while your reputation is blackened, find yourself a prisoner of the computer. Today, hundreds of thousands of Americans are losing. They don't know how to play the credit card game—to win. This book tells *you* how.

The first thing to do is be sure you know the rules. You've been using credit cards for years, so you think you know them. Maybe. But currently the credit card services are being sued for upwards of $1 billion dollars by irate card holders who claim some of the rules were changed in mid-stream and nobody ever told them. Fact is, in recent years—particularly since the banks began their big-time invasion of credit card country—many of the rules of the credit card game *have* been changed, with or without notice. And these are the rules you've got to know before you can profit from the "hidden" advantages of the credit card, and sidestep the "hidden" booby traps. So here's a brief refresher on how the credit card game is being played right now. The facts that follow will come in handy when you begin to play *your* cards.

*   *   *

The object of the game—what is it? Or, putting it another way, why do you use credit cards in the first place?

Life magazine has an answer: They're a "dreamy method of buying by signature after the money has run out." The owner of a posh restaurant is more direct: "My customers use credit cards so they can buy meals they can't afford." A travel agency advertises: "Play now. Pay later." One retailer told us: "It's the only way millions of people can afford big-ticket [high priced] items. They never could put lump sums on the barrelhead."

It all adds up to this: You use credit cards because you want all the fine things that America can produce, and all the fine services that America can offer, and you just don't have the free cash with which to buy them. "We were forced into the credit card business," says Kenneth S. Axelson, director of finance of J. C. Penney's multi-billion dollar retail empire, "by consumers who kept asking for . . . credit."

But getting, as one bank advertises, "everything you ever dreamed of" on the cuff is not the whole appeal of the credit card.

Many women who can afford to pay cash tell us that the greatest advantage of the credit card comes when they return merchandise. "When you pay cash," one veteran shopper reports, "even the better stores give you an argument when you ask for your money back. But when you return anything on a credit card purchase, you always get full credit for what you bought, and no questions asked. That's a pretty wonderful thing, because you know how we women like to take things back."

A truck driver answered our question, "Why do you use credit cards?" with: "Like everybody else, you don't have the cash now, but you'll have it later, so you pay when you have it. But there's another thing—I don't like to write a lot of checks at the end of the month. If I can write one check for a lot of bills, that makes me happy. So I get my wife and the grown-up kids to use my credit cards."

"I use credit cards," a housewife confessed, "because when I say 'Charge it,' it gives *me* a charge. You know, you feel great. Important. Like you've arrived. Something very special happens to me when I use a credit card."

"You know something," a young man confided, "I read somewhere that with my credit cards I can buy anything I want in 500,000 places all over the world. I can take off for Tokyo, stop at the Imperial Hotel, and be wined and dined by Geisha girls—and I don't have to take a cent with me. That makes me feel like—wow, man—like Rockefeller."

Simplifying some of the chores of modern living, and satisfying psychological as well as economic needs, the credit card has become a way of life. With a booming impact on the economy. Surveys show that Americans spend 23 percent more using a credit card than they do using cash. J. C. Penney's gross sales hovered around $600 million on a strictly cash-and-carry basis, but "This year," boasts the company's finance chief, "we expect more than $1 billion of merchandise will be purchased through our credit plans." There are currently more than 260 million credit cards in circulation, racking up yearly purchases in excess of $12 billion. Retailers' dependence on this credit system, comments a spokesman for the Practicing Law Institute in a recent seminar on consumer credit, "is like our dependence on electric power . . . enormous. Take the system away . . . " and the nation's stores black out. But keep the power flowing and the nation prospers. And so do you— in continued employment, in greater fringe benefits, in higher wages, in more money with which to make more credit purchases and re-charge the economy to greater prosperity.

Why do you play the credit-card game?

To live the good life.

And a better one.

*   *   *

What kind of cards do you use to play the credit card game? There are four basic kinds. Three of them are free.

That is to say, you pay no fee for the use of these cards. One kind requires a fee. Here's a run-down:

FREE. COMPANY CARDS. These are charge account cards issued by business organizations for use only in the outlets of the organizations. Example: A Macy's C-T card. You can use it in any of the Macy's branches, but not in Gimbels. Cards of this type are issued mostly by department stores, mail order houses, chains, discount houses and specialty shops. Some oil company credit cards fall into this category, some hotel chain cards, and some airline cards.

Hint: Many formerly for-use-in-our-outlets-only type cards now take in more territory. If you've had a card of this type for some time, ask for the most recent literature. You may have a surprise in store.

FREE. COMPANY CARDS PLUS. These are company cards issued by business organizations for use in their own outlets *and* in other outlets. Good examples are the oil company credit cards. They're also good examples of how for-use-in-our-outlets-only type cards are transformed into cards accepted by other-than-company outlets as well. Here's the story:

Oil company credit cards were conceived—some as long ago as the early 1900's—as an aid to the gas station dealer. He owned the station, but what with buying gas and oil, and paying help, and drawing money to live on, he didn't have anything left over to finance consumer credit. Nor did he want to take a chance on being stuck with bad debts. But in the fierce competition for the motorist's dollar, credit was a high-octane lure, so the oil companies came to the dealer's rescue. "We wanted to eliminate his risk in extending credit," one oil company spokesman relates, "and eliminate the burden of the investment." When a motorist used an oil company credit card, the oil company paid the dealer, then collected later from the motorist. What the oil company got in return from the dealer was an agreement to use only *that* oil company's products. So it was only in *that* oil company's outlets that its credit card was good.

With virtually all the major oil companies offering credit cards, the competition for the motorist's dollar became the competition for his credit dollar, and each oil company vied to make its credit card the most attractive. One way: By extending the number of places it could be used and, therefore, the variety of goods and services that could be charged with it. The Mobil credit card now buys not only gas, oil, tires, batteries and minor repairs, but also food and lodging in thousands of motels all over the country, as well as transportation on sea and in air.

Because of similar competitive pressures, airlines have also expanded the use of their consumer credit cards. Pan Am's card, for instance, is now good for travel on other airlines, too, and is honored by car rental services, airport restaurants, hotels, travel agents, and duty-free shops in whatever country Pan Am "makes the going great." If you're stranded in a strange port without cash, the Pan Am card can even get you $50 in local currency.

Any company card is likely to offer much the same basic pluses as any other company card in its field (as soon as one card innovates, the rest of them imitate). Result: To attract your credit card business, companies from time to time add special allurements to their cards. One oil company offers you fine china at cut price—with its card. One airline card underwrites your medical expenses abroad. One mail order house is planning to introduce "buying-from-your-home" by means of push-button closed circuit TV—exclusive for company card holders, of course. All these specials are like "loss leaders" in the supermarket. The companies lose money on them in order to lead you to charge much more. Like any wise shopper, take advantage of the specials. Caution: Don't let them lead you into charging too much more. That's one way to lose the game.

FREE. BANK CARDS. These are credit cards issued by banks, and they're far more versatile than company credit cards. You can buy more kinds of goods and services with them, you can use them in more outlets. Just one statistic: You can charge with your BankAmericard in more than 600,000 outlets in the continental United States alone. However, be careful when you pick up a card in your local bank: If it's a *local* bank card (that is to say, *not* your local bank's version of a BankAmericard, Master Charge card, or Uni-Card), it's only going to be honored by local merchants. No real drawback, because you're going to do most of your shopping with them anyway. Ever since the local bank card was introduced by the Franklin National Bank of New York in 1951, consumers have thought it was a real fine service. More than 20 million local bank card holders think so now.

But although there are more than a thousand banks offering their own cards today, the chances are that the number will diminish sizeably in the next few years. Local banks find it far more convenient, and far less expensive, to issue credit cards from one of the two international credit card systems, BankAmericard and Master Charge. These systems franchise their cards to the nation's banks, much as fried chicken, bowling alleys, motels, and Howard Johnson's are franchised. For a fee, the systems supply all the know-how, merchandising and machinery for processing the cards (including the multi-million dollar computer complexes), and the local banks put the cards "on the air" (that's bankers' slang for "distribute them by mail whether you want them or not") and reap the profits from the credit card windfall. You profit when you use these cards because you can charge in all the States of the Union and in all the major cities abroad.

Your chances of getting a BankAmericard and/or a Master Charge card are good no matter where you live or work. More than 3,000 banks are now franchised to handle Bank-Americards and almost as many have signed up with Master Charge. Multiply the number of banks by the number of branches in each bank, and you get more than 10,000 bank offices where you can pick up your BankAmericard or Master Charge card. Odds are, one of those offices is near you. So widespread are these two franchise operations that you may already be one of the 41 million Americans who charge up an average $185 a month each on these cards. If you're not, expansion programs of these two bank credit card giants indicate you may soon be.

There's a third major bank card system, but it's regional. This is Uni-Card. It's issued by three banks, and honors charges in nine states from Maine to Pennsylvania. These three banks have about 100 branches, more than 30,000 merchants honor the card, and nearly 2 million consumers carry it. Although scarcely comparable in size to its two massive competitors, and restricted to a corner of the nation, Uni-Card may still have an influence on your credit card game in the future, no matter where you live. There are several reasons for this:

For one thing, Uni-Card has demonstrated a tough capacity for survival despite the onslaughts of its two powerful adversaries. It's been around (allowing for a brief span when it was temporarily taken out of circulation) as long as Bank-Americard, and longer than Master Charge. The Chase Manhattan Bank's "Charge Plan," which was the parent of today's Uni-Card was launched about 1958-59, around the same time that California's Bank of America began to develop BankAmericard. Master Charge took shape a year or two later when several San Francisco banks reacted to the explosive growth that the credit card had triggered at the Bank of America.)

For another, Uni-Card has been consistently inventive. (Its sponsor, the Chase Manhattan Bank, is one of the nation's most creative financial institutions. To its credit, for example, is the introduction of payment of daily interest to savings depositors.) Currently, Uni-Card offers certain exclusive insurance features to protect the loser against loss and theft. It also allows a merchant to issue a Uni-Card in the merchant's name alone. For example: It's *Allenby's* Credit Card, not Allenby's Uni-Card—and none of the other systems permits this. Those electronic box offices, Ticketrons, have been installed in many Chase Manhattan branches, and you can charge your ducats to concerts, sporting events, and theatres with Uni-Card—but no other card.

Durable, and always in the forefront of credit card progress, Uni-Card may expand its territory in the near future. More likely though, Uni-Card will ultimately merge with one or another of the two mammoth systems. But if it does, it will bring its own special expertise into the merger. When you play your cards tomorrow, you may be able to rake in one or two extra tricks because it did. In the meantime though, if you're in Chase Manhattan country, add a Uni-Card to your hand.

NOT FREE. T&E CARDS. The "T" and "E" stand for *T*ravel and *E*ntertainment. T&E cards are the Cadillacs of the credit card industry. They originated after World War II, primarily as an accounting device; an expense account record that couldn't be disputed even by the sourest of company treasurers or the most suspicious of tax investigators—so they were meant for the big spenders. Because of the well-heeled clientele (most of the tabs were picked up not by individuals, but by their big corporation employers) and because of the blue-sky credit ceilings ($10,000 and up, up and away), posh restaurants and the finest hotels were quick to make T&E decals part of their decor—and their lure. Luxury stores got on the gilt-edged bandwagon fast, and soon there was very little that was fashionable, hard-to-get, or expensive that you couldn't buy with T&E cards—from an unblended 1908 cognac at dinner to a suite at the Waldorf. You could even buy people. Explanation: Outfits like Manpower and Staff Builders supply temporary help of all kinds, and with your Diners' Club card, you could buy the services of a secretary from them, or hire a financial consultant or a clown for a children's party. You can see why the possession of a T&E card carries so much prestige.

For a long time—say from 1950 to 1965, the year the mass invasion of bank credit cards began—T&E cards were *the* credit cards. So today, despite the varieties of credit cards available, when you say, "credit card," you think, *"T&E credit card."* When you carry any credit card, you feel as important as if you were carrying one of the prestige cards. Plunk down any plastic, and you too become a member of the expense account elite—not only in your mind, but also in the minds of the people who pick up your card. It's all quite real, this puffing of your ego on credit—and it's the T&E cards that have done it for you.

Today, T&E cards still retain their aura of red carpets and champagne breakfasts, but their appeal has been broadened to combat an up-tight economy and the unrelenting competition of other multi-outlet credit card systems. Diners' Club was the first multi-outlet credit card system in the U.S.A., but now it has to fight off 49 others. It was founded in 1950 with an investment of $18,000, billed $500 million dollars a decade later, made a $2.6 million profit as late as 1967, but dropped $23 million in fiscal 1970. The T&E card companies now have to get into the donnybrook for your credit card dollar, and they're using the same tactics as all the other credit card services: They're making the cards easier for you to get, offering you more when you get them.

You get a T&E card these days if you're earning as little as $7,200 a year. The average family income is $8,500. T&E card companies don't care if you're an executive, or whether you know the difference between Beluga and Sevruga caviar, they want your business no matter who you are. Result: Your Diners' Club, or American Express or Carte Blanche card is as likely to be honored in your friendly neighborhood restaurant as it is in a haute cuisine establishment. You can shop with any of them as easily on Main Street as on Fifth Avenue. You get "attractive and unusual gifts . . . immediate guarantee of credit at over 1,300 hospitals in all 50 states . . . low cost group accidental death insurance . . . credit card protection against loss, theft and fraud"—and one T&E company, riding on the tide of the Women's Lib movement, gives *"her* credit for being a woman [with] an exclusive pink and gold HERS card."

When you get your T&E card, you'll be joining about six million other Americans who each ante up $15 a year to enjoy the new pluses of the prestige cards as well as two stick-out advantages remaining from the cards' golden days. One: T&E cards will be accepted in some of the better shops and restaurants that still hold out against accepting bank cards. Two: There's virtually no ceiling to what you can charge on a T&E card. It's those advantages that put T&E cards in the Cadillac class. And it's those advantages that keep them there.

*   *   *

That's it. Four different kinds of cards. Fifty different multi-outlet card systems. Thousands of franchised cards. And well over 10,000 different cards issued by individual banks and stores. What can you buy with them? Almost anything from kumquats to a complete office staff. In some states, you can use credit cards to pay taxes. In New York City, if Howard Samuels, the commissioner of off-track betting has his way, you'll soon be able to buy your parimutuel tickets with credit cards. Credit cards will even buy you money. Except for retail store cards, most credit cards permit cash advances or guarantee your personal check (if your check bounces, the credit card service pays off). Best cards for raising money are bank cards. A Master Charge card, for example, can get you as much as $500 in hard currency with no questions asked. One credit card calls itself *The New Money*. Another, *The Everything Card*. Put the two slogans together and you've got the picture.

*   *   *

How do you get these cards? No problem. Fact is, bank cards are more often than not wafted to you seductively in the mail whether you want them or not. If you're not one of the "lucky" recipients and you want to get one of these cards, it's as simple as writing your name, address, spouse's name, telephone number, place of employment and one or two other bits of data on an application form. If you've been working fairly steadily and you haven't been flitting about the country, you'll get the plastic. You may have to meet certain special requirements like: T&E card companies say "no" if you're not earning at least $140 a week; oil companies would like to know that you own a car. Standards of acceptance vary from card issuer to card issuer but, on the whole, demands are minimal, red tape has been cut to shreds, and everything is done to get the card into your hands as rapidly as possible; whether it's a bank card or any other type of plastic. Provided —and this is a big proviso—your credit slate is clean. *They* know if it's not—you can thank the computers for that—and if it's not, you just won't get a card. A word of advice: *Keep your credit slate clean.* If you don't, the computer can black-ball you forever, anywhere, faster than you can say, "Charge."

If you have a good credit history with one card, you'll have even less trouble getting other cards. There is now more than one card in circulation for every living American. Some consumers carry as many as 40 to 60 cards. Few card carriers hold less than six. If you're an average credit card user, your wallet is stuffed with about 20 cards.

*   *   *

What'll it cost you to play your cards? That is to say: What'll it cost over the cost of the goods and services you purchase?

On *free* cards, there need be no extra cost at all. All free cards give you between 25 to 30 days from the date you're billed to pay up without any interest or carrying charge added to the purchase price. "Finance charges"—in good old-fashion-ed banking language, interest—doesn't begin until after those 25-30 days. So pay up before then and your free cards are really free.

After those 25-30 days grace however, you're soaked with interest costs on your unpaid balance. Most rates are 18 percent per year (1½ percent per month) on balances under $500, and 12 percent per year (1 percent per month) on balances over $500. That's when you charge goods and services. When you charge cash, you pay only 12 percent per year no matter what amount you borrow, but you get no free credit days; interest begins from the day you draw the money. The interest rate on cash advances is generally the same in all 50 states, but there are some variations in interest rates for goods and services charged on your credit cards. If, for example, in Montana, you've charged up a vacation and a TV set, and your balance is over $300, you pay only 7 percent per year on the amount that's over—and that's the lowest credit card interest rate in the nation. Here's a chart that shows:

WHERE CREDIT CARD
INTEREST RATES ARE LOWER

States	Unpaid Balance*	Monthly Rate	Yearly Rate
Ariz., Ark., Idaho	All	5/6%	10%
Ind., Wash.	All	1%	12%
N.J., Wisc.	All	1%	12%
Penn.	$500 or less	1¼%	15%
Ohio	Over $400	1%	12%
Kansas	Over $300	1%	12%
Colo.	$300 or less	1¼%	15%
Colo.	Over $300	5/6%	10%
Missouri	Over $500	3/4%	9%
Montana	$300 or less	11/12%	11%
Montana	Over $300	7/12%	7%

Paying interest, you can take advantage of what the credit card sales promotion literature calls "extended payment." That means you can extend your payments for about three years (that's when credit card services request 10 percent of your *unpaid* balance—*not* 10 percent of your total purchase—each time payment is due). You can take even longer to pay. Some credit card services have slashed that "10 percent of unpaid balance" down to a bit more than 4 percent: *All you have to pay is 1/24 of what you owe* at payment time. On these terms,

---

* *Where balance is not specified, rates are 18 percent per year up to $500, 12 percent per year over $500.*

depending on the size of your bill, it could take six years or more before you're through paying. But even six years *is not* forever. However, you *can* keep paying forever. Here's why:

As soon as you've paid off a monthly installment, you can go out and charge again. Now you have a new balance, and another three to six years to pay it off. Pay off and charge the next month, and you still have three to six years to pay. Month after month you can do the same thing and still have the same stretch of unpaid installments ahead of you. It's as if money to pay off your debts was whirling out one door while, at the same time, new debts were whirling in another door. Your credit situation is like a revolving door. And that's what credit card companies mean when they invite you to use their "revolving" credit. It is, unquestionably, a useful consumer credit device: It permits you to buy the things you need while you're still in debt. But be careful: Once you're caught in the revolving door of credit, you could be in a spin for the rest of your life.

There's no revolving credit or extended credit on T&E cards (although you can arrange for them on request). Big selling point of the T&E card is the claim that there's never an interest charge. But the fact is, there *is* an interest charge. It's simply hidden. Follow this arithmetic: Suppose you spend $50 a month with your T&E card. But to get $50 free of interest for one month, you have to pay for your card. That's $15 a year, or $1.25 a month ($15 divided by 12 months). Divide $1.25 by $50 and you get 2½ percent—which is the monthly "interest" rate. Multiply that monthly rate by the twelve months of the year, and the annual "interest" you're paying on your T&E card comes to—*30 percent!* Of course, the greater the amount of your purchases, the lower the interest rate figures to be. For example, if your purchases come to $100 a month (not $50), your annual "interest" rate is

15 percent (not 30). You *can* use a bank card without paying interest, but on everything you buy with a T&E card, you have to figure in the cost of the hidden interest.

*   *   *

Now you know all the basic rules of the credit card game. You know why you need credit cards, what kinds there are, what you can charge with them, how you get them, and how much they'll cost you. Play the game according to the rules and you can live better than any average man in the history of the world—even though you can afford to live only 1/24 as well. Learn the fine points, as we'll teach them to you in the pages that follow, and you can turn your plastics into gold. All without risk.

In the old wonder tales, the locked door to fabulous treasures burst open when the words, "Open, sesame," were uttered. Today, the word is—

Charge!

CHAPTER II

How to Make Money on Money You've Already Spent

Use the right combination of credit cards at the right time, and you can get up to 90 days to pay—without interest or carrying charges. So why not use that money to make more money? Here's how to spend your money and keep it, too—for as long as three months. And here's how to earn more than 7 percent on the money you've already spent.

Charge!

But don't pay for as long as you can get away with it without interest, penalties, or even a cross note from a computer. That's about two months on bank cards (and other cards with bank-type extended credit features), and three months on T&E cards—with the full approval of the credit card services. Naturally, they don't go out of their way to tell you how to do it—but it's all there in the rules and regulations for payments, and in the way you're billed. It's just a matter of figuring it out. Follow us as we figure it out with you.

Let's start with your bank card.

You make a purchase with it on Monday, some time between store opening and 2:30 in the afternoon. Before 3 P.M., your retailer deposits your charge slip in his bank. It's the same bank from which you got your credit card. The bank *at once* credits the amount of your purchase (less the bank's fee) to your retailer's account. So on the same Monday that you made the charge, your retailer has been paid by the bank. But the bank does not chalk up the cost to your credit card account on that Monday.

The bank sends your charge slip to its Service Processing Center to be recorded and computerized. That takes at least a day. You're not charged with a cent during that time. It's Tuesday before the charge goes on your account. So your *Real* Charge Date is one day *after* you've made the charge.

Make the purchase on Monday *after* 3 P.M., the end of the bank's day, and even if your merchant makes a late deposit that day, your charge slip is not sent to the bank's Service Processing Center until Tuesday, and by the time it's recorded, it's Wednesday. Your *Real* Charge Date is two days after you've made the charge.

If *your* bank (that is, the bank that issued your credit card) is not the same as your retailer's bank, then your charge slip has to be sent from *his* bank to *your* bank—and that takes still another day. If you made the purchase on Monday after 3 P.M., you wouldn't be charged for it until Thursday. Your *Real* Charge Date is three days after you've made the charge.

Make that Monday afternoon purchase *out of town,* and the out-of-town bank has to send your charge slip to the proper Processing Service Center, which in turn has to send it on to your bank, and that eats up time. On out-of-town charges, your *Real* Charge Date is about five to six days after you've made the charge. (And it *can* be longer. We know of a case where it took more than 20 days for a charge made in Virginia to be debited to an account in New York.)

But what we've been talking about are *working* days. When holidays or weekends are involved, your *Real* Charge Date is even further removed from the date on which you made the charge. Example: Make a purchase on Wednesday after 3 P.M., at a retailer whose bank is *not* the same as yours. That means your *Real* Charge Date is three days later. But

three days later is a Saturday, and the banks are closed and
will stay closed for two days. The next working day is Monday. *That's* your *Real* Charge Date, and that's five (3+2)
days after the date you made the charge. Therefore:

To determine your Real *Charge Date, add the number of
days the banks are closed while your charge slip is being
processed, to the number of working days it takes to record
your charge.*

Here's the whole business of calculating your *Real* Charge
Date in an easy-to-use-chart:

REAL CHARGE DATE CHART

A	B	C	D	E
local	same bank	before 3 P.M.	1	
		after 3 P.M.	2	
	different bank	before 3 P.M.	2	+ number of days banks are closed
		after 3 P.M.	3	
out of town	different bank	before 3 P.M.	5	
		after 3 P.M.	6	

Here's how to use the chart:

Go down column A and check off whether you're dealing
with a local charge or an out-of-town (not suburban) charge.
Go to column B, and pick the line that applies; if your bank
and your retailer's bank are the same, use the line reading
"same bank"; if they're different, use the line reading "different bank." (Caution: By same bank, we don't mean the same
branch of a bank, but the same banking institution. For example: First National City Bank has hundreds of branches.
If your bank card was issued by a First National City Bank,
and your retailer's Master Charge account is with a First

National City Bank, you and your retailer have the *same* bank, even though you may have your accounts in different branches. To find the name of your retailer's bank, look at the charge slip; it's often on it. If it's not, ask him.)

Now go to column C on the line you've just chosen—same or different bank—and put your finger on either the top line, if you've made your purchase before 3 P.M., or on the bottom line, if you've made your purchase after 3 P.M. (Fine point: Although it's not likely that your retailer will deposit a charge slip made out after 2:30, it's possible, so be on the safe side, don't figure a purchase made at 2:30 as a purchase made after 3 P.M.) Then carry your finger over to the corresponding line in column D. This gives you the number of working days from the day you make the charge to the day the charge appears on your account. Next to that number, insert in column E the number of days the banks are closed within the time it takes to record your charge. Add the numbers in column D and column E, and you get the total number of days from the date you made your purchase to the *Real* Charge Date.

Example: You make a charge locally. Your bank is different than your retailer's. You make the charge after 3 P.M. The day after you make the charge is the start of a three day holiday. Your chart looks like this:

REAL CHARGE DATE CHART

A	B	C	D	E
(local)	same bank	before 3 P.M. after 3 P.M.	1 2	
	(different) bank	before 3 P.M. (after 3 P.M.)	2 (3)	+3 (number of days banks are closed) =6
out of town	different bank	before 3 P.M. after 3 P.M.	5 6	

If your charge was made on the 1st, your *Real* Charge Date is 6 days later, or the 7th.

Caution: The *Real* Charge Date chart is intended to supply basic guidelines. It's up to you to *experience* the *actual* time between charge and *Real* Charge Date. They may be shorter than the times we've given you. They may be longer. Adjust *your* chart accordingly.

* * *

Now that you know *how* to calculate your *Real* Charge Date, let's see *why* you have to know that date to extend your free credit days to a maximum.

Take this case: You have a *billing date* of the 30th. That means the bank bills you once a month for charges accrued during the month, and the bill comes to you dated the 30th. This bill includes all charges entered on your account up to the end of business on the 30th. You don't have to pay any of these charges for 25 days after your billing date. After 25 days, interest begins to mount up at 12 to 18 percent in most states. So you start with 25 days free credit.

Example: If you make a local charge *before* 3 P.M. on the 29th, a Monday when Tuesday isn't a holiday, and your bank is the same as your retailer's, your *Real* Charge Date is *one* day later. That's the 30th. But your billing date is the 30th, so the charge will appear on the bill of the 30th, and you'll have to pay it 25 days later.

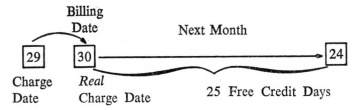

But suppose you made the purchase *after* 3 P.M. on the 29th. Then your *Real* Charge Date (see *Real* Charge Date Chart) is now *two* days later, or the 31st.

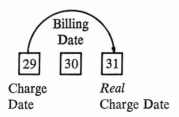

You'll have skipped over the billing date. The charge will not appear until the next billing date—

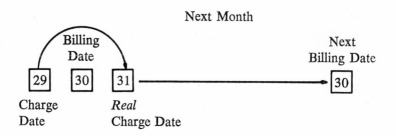

which is 30 days hence. And you won't have to pay for another 25 days.

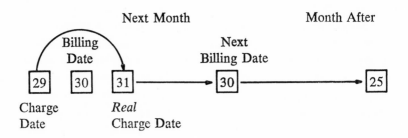

You get 55 free credit days *plus* the two days between charge date and *Real* Charge Date, for a total of 57 free credit days. By simply shifting your charge from before 3 P.M. to after 3 P.M., you gain 32 additional days of free credit. But you can get even more.

Refer back to the *Real* Charge Date, column D, and you'll find that (not taking weekends or holidays into account) you can charge locally as long as *three* days before the 31st to skip over your billing date.

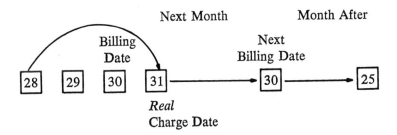

That extends your free credit days to 58.

Make your purchases out of town, and column D of the *Real* Charge Date chart tells you that you can go back as much as *six* working days before the 31st to skip over your billing date. But six working days must include one or two weekends, so that gives you two or four more free credit days. You now have eight or ten *extra* free credit days. Add them to the 55 free credit days you get by skipping over your billing date, and you'll find that you don't have to pay on out-of-town purchases for 63 to 65 days. Caution: Often on out-of-town purchases, you can charge even further back than six days and still skip over the billing date. But that's a gamble. Figure six days and play it safe.

So by skipping over your billing date, you're able to extend your free credit days on bank cards to about two months. You skip over your billing date when you charge *before* your billing date *but on such dates and at such times to insure that your charges won't appear on your account until* after *your billing date.* And that's why you must know how to calculate your *Real* Charge Date.

*   *   *

But achieving about two months free credit by the method we've just described has a serious drawback. You can only do your shopping in the days immediately *before* your billing date. You can, however, get an equivalent amount of free credit in the week *following* your billing date without taking the *Real* Charge Date into account at all. If, for example, you do your shopping on the 31st:

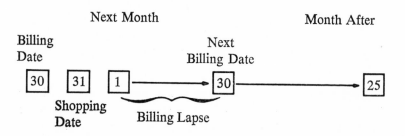

Because of the *billing lapse,* the charge doesn't show up on your bill until the 30th of the following month. You don't have to pay for it until 25 days after that. This gives you a total of 55 free credit days. Make your purchases on the first and you get 54 days; on the second, 53 days; on the third 52 days, and so on. The least amount of free credit time you get during the week is 49 days, which isn't bad. (There's no special advantage about making out-of-town purchases during this week since, even if the *Real* Charge Date were 20 days later, the charges would still be chalked up by the 27th, early enough to make the billing date of the 30th.)

Taking advantage of the *Real* Charge Date in the week *before* your billing date, and of the *billing lapse* in the week *after* your billing date, you can get about two month's free credit in two weeks out of a month. But by combining the *Real* Charge Date method with the *billing lapse* method— *and adding a few more bank cards to your hand*—you can get two months' free credit *anytime during the month*. Here's how:

Take the month of October. Your billing date is the 30th. You know that you can charge as early as the 28th locally and the 22nd out of town in order to skip over your billing date. In the calendar below, the billing date is indicated by a shadowed box, and the shopping dates on which you can use the *Real* Charge Date method are indicated by arrows.

M	T	W	Th.	F	Sat.	Sun.
			1	2	3	4
5	6	7	8	9	10	11
12	13	14	15	16	17	18
19	20	21	22	23	24	25
26	27	28	29	30	31	

Now let's suppose you have an *additional* billing date (the billing date of one of the bank cards you've just added to your hand). Say it's the 22nd. Then:

M	T	W	Th.	F	Sat.	Sun.
			1	2	3	4
5	6	7	8	9	10	11
12	13	14	15	16	17	18
19	20	21	22	23	24	25
26	27	28	29	30	31	

Now you can use the *Real* Charge Date method for half the month. Add *two more* billing dates (of two additional bank cards) on the 15th and on the 7th and—

M	T	W	Th.	F	Sat.	Sun.
			1	2	3	4
5	6	7	8	9	10	11
12	13	14	15	16	17	18
19	20	21	22	23	24	25
26	27	28	29	30	31	

you're covered for the *entire month*.

Can you get four different billing dates? Not on one bank card. (If you could, you wouldn't want it; instead of paying every month, you'd be paying every week.) But you can get four different bank cards each with different billing dates. Can you get the billing dates you want: the 7th, 15th, 22nd and 30th? (The dates need not be the 7th, 15th, 22nd and

30th; all you need is four billing dates seven to eight days apart.) Nothing's easier. Here's why:

To ease their bookkeeping load, banks bill out some of their cards *every working date of the month.* Any date can be your billing date, and the banks make a selling point of letting you pick the date most convenient to you. If you're getting a new card, pick one of the four dates necessary for two month's free credit. If you have bank cards now that don't bear any of these four dates, ask your banks to change your billing dates. They'll do it gladly. They'll even provide "billing date change forms" that will help you get it done without fuss or feathers.

But the four dates will give you complete coverage only if you make out-of-town purchases as well as local purchases. If you restrict yourself to local purchases, as most of us do, then the coverage you're able to obtain by use of the *Real* Charge Date method is limited to these dates:

M	T	W	Th.	F	Sat.	Sun.
			1	2	3	4
5	6	7	8	9	10	11
12	13	14	15	16	17	18
19	20	21	22	23	24	25
26	27	28	29	30	31	

But remember, during the week *after* each billing date, you can obtain two months' free credit by taking advantage of the *billing lapse.* By combining the two methods, you're covered for every day.

How do you know which card to use? Obviously, you use the card with the billing date most distant from the $\overline{Real}$ Charge Date.

Example: You make a local purchase on Friday the 9th after 3 P.M. You and your retailer use different banks. Your *Real* Charge Date (see *Real* Charge Date chart) is three working days plus the weekend, or five days from the 9th. That's the 14th. Of the four cards that you have, don't use the one with the billing date of the 15th, that's only one day away; nor of the 22nd, that's only eight days away; nor of the 30th, that's only 16 days away; but of the *7th* because that's the 7th of *next* month, and that's 24 days away. Tack the bank's 25 days of free credit on to that 24, and add the five days between the day you charged, the 9th, and the *Real* Charge Date, the 14th, and you get 54 free credit days. So you use the credit card with the billing date of the 7th.

Another example: You make your purchase locally at 11 A.M. on Wednesday, the 21st. You and your retailer use the same bank. From the *Real* Charge Date chart, you calculate your *Real* Charge Date as the 22nd. The card with the most distant billing date is the card with the billing date of the 15th *of next month*. Use it. Your free credit days add up to 24 (from the 22nd to the 15th of next month), plus 25 (the bank's regular free credit period), plus one day gained from charge date to *Real* Charge Date. That's a total of 50 free credit days.

You can see that the total amount of free credit days you get varies. If you want to shop only on those days in which you get the *most* free credit days, repeat the calculations used in the two examples we've just given you for *every* day of the month. Then make your purchases on those days that produce the longest free credit periods. *A rule of thumb: You get the longest free credit periods by charging in the days immediately before a billing date. The second longest free credit periods are obtainable on the billing date and immediately after.* So the more billing dates you have, the more days will be available during which you can obtain maximum free credit periods. And you can get more billing dates simply by carrying more cards.

*   *   *

Two months then, give or take a few days, is about as much free credit time as you can expect on a bank card. The same is true of other free cards: company cards, transportation cards, hotel cards, and the rest. But you can get more free credit days on T&E cards. There are two reasons.

The first: The time between the date you make the charge and the date the charge appears on your account is longer than the time between those two dates when you use bank cards. (T&E billing is more centralized than banks', and it takes more time to get your charge slips to the centralized computer billing center.) That gives you a few more days of free credit.

The second, and by far the more important reason: Instead of giving you 25 days from billing date to pay, T&E card services give you up to 60 days. That's another month's free credit. Use the same methods to extend your free credit periods that you used with your bank cards and *you can get about three months free credit with your T&E cards.* (*Caution*: *Real* Charge Dates on T&E cards are not the same as on bank cards. T&E card services don't follow banking timetables: the 3 P.M. deadline, for example, is meaningless. Just how long it takes before the charge actually appears on your account is something you'll have to determine from your own experience.)

In a nutshell then, here's how to get the maximum number of free credit days on your credit cards, whether they're free cards or T&E cards.

1. Obtain at least four credit cards, each with a different billing date.
2. When you make a charge, calculate the *Real* Charge Date.
3. Use the credit card which gives you the most distant billing date from the *Real* Charge Date.

Hint: You can squeeze out more free time on both bank and T&E cards by not paying quite on time. If you're late, banks and most free card services have the right to charge you interest. However, experience has shown that if payment arrives a few days past the due date, *provided the payment is in full,* no interest charges are levied. Those few extra days can be stretched out to a week or two on T&E card payments.

*   *   *

By making use of the four card method to extend your free credit days to the maximum, you can earn money on money you've already spent. Put yourself in the following situation.

Until now, you've cashed your payroll check and used the cash during the coming week to make your purchases. Your cash expenditures average $100 a week. Now switch to charge, averaging $20 per day, Monday through Friday. You have four credit cards. Billing dates are the same as before, the 7th, 15th, 22nd and 30th. You get paid weekly on Fridays.

PAY DAY

M	T	W	Th.	F	Sat.	Sun.
				25	26	27
28	29	30	1	2	3	4
5	6	7	8	9	10	11
12	13	14	15	16	17	18
19	20	21	22	23	24	25
26	27	28	29	30	31	

Here's what you do. On Friday, the 25th, deposit $100 from your paycheck, in a day of deposit to day of withdrawal savings account paying 5 percent interest. During the following week, ending Friday, the 2nd, charge up $100. On Friday, the 2nd, deposit another $100 in your savings account.

You begin the next week with $200 in your account. During that week, from Monday, the 5th, through Friday, the 10th, you charge $100. Use the card with the most distant billing date to give you the most distant due date. As you already know, this is the card with the billing date of the 7th. On Friday, the 10th, deposit another $100 in your account. You now have $300 on deposit, and your charges total $200.

Repeat this procedure week after week, making sure that you always use the card with the most distant billing date. You may have to change cards in the middle of the week. For example, on Monday, the 26th, you'll be using your card with a billing date of the 22nd, but on Tuesday, the 27th, or Wednesday, the 28th, you'll have to switch to your card with a billing date of the 30th.

By the sixth week, you'll have piled up $700 in your account, and you'll owe $600 in charges. In this week, your first billing date is reached.

DEPOSIT
DAYS

NUMBER OF WEEKS	M	T	W	Th	F	Sat	Sun
					25	26	27
1	28	29	30	1	2	3	4
2	5	6	7	8	9	10	11
3	12	13	14	15	16	17	18
4	19	20	21	22	23	24	25
5	26	27	28	29	30	31	1
6	2	3	4	5	6	7	8

You'll be required to pay 25 days thereafter.

DEPOSIT
DAYS

NUMBER OF WEEKS	M	T	W	Th	F	Sat	Sun
6	2	3	4	5	6	7	8
7	9	10	11	12	13	14	15
8	16	17	18	19	20	21	22
9	23	24	25	26	27	28	29
10	30	1	2				

By the time you're called upon to make your first payment of $100, ten Fridays will have passed, and you'll have made ten deposits of $100 each for a total of $1,000. On the payment date, you withdraw $100, leaving $900 on deposit. Your next billing date is the 15th of November, and you have to pay for that bill on the 10th of December, in the 11th week. By this time, you'll have deposited another $100, so when you withdraw the $100 you have to pay, your balance will remain at $900.

As you continue week after week to charge and deposit, your balance will average out to over $900. At 5%, compounded daily from date of deposit to date of withdrawal, that's about $47 a year.

You can increase your yield by depositing your savings, the money you've already spent but which is making money for you, in a two year savings certificate paying 6 percent. But the use of a savings certificate has a serious shortcoming. Your money is tied up for two years. Should you need that money in the meantime, you'll regret locking it away for only an additional one percent. Particularly when there's a new way to earn as much as 7 percent or more, and still be able to withdraw part or all of your funds whenever you like.

The way is by putting your savings in the Mutual Fund for Investing in U. S. Government Securities, Inc.* The fund does not deal in common stocks or corporate bonds, but only in, according to its prospectus, "a diversified portfolio of U. S. Government securities." Guaranteed by the U. S. Government, the portfolio is safer than the investment and loan portfolios of any bank or Savings and Loan Association in the country. It is currently paying at the rate of 7.2 percent per year, with interest accrued daily. Just one drawback: There's a small sales charge (maximum 1½ percent). So for

---

The Fund's address is 423 Seventh Avenue, Pittsburgh, Pa. 15219.

savings that will probably be withdrawn within eight or nine months, you're better off sticking to your 5% savings account. If you think you can get along without withdrawing for longer than nine months, then this new way of saving should be attractive since it combines safety, high return, and ready availability of funds.

Charging $100 a week, you can pick up an additional income of about $67 a year when you place the money you've already spent, but didn't have to pay, in the Mutual Fund for Investing in U. S. Government Securities, Inc. That's figured on the basis of using bank cards with a maximum free credit period of about two months. Use T&E cards instead, and you gain another month. That extra month gives you more money to invest. This can push up your income on a charge of $100 a week to about $100 a year. Careful, though: The cost of each T&E card reduces the yield. Only if your charges average over $500 per month are the T&E cards more profitable to you.

*   *   *

To make money with your credit cards then, just take these two simple steps:

Step One. Get the maximum free credit days on your charges by using at least four credit cards, and selecting for use those cards with the most distant billing dates.

Step Two. Put the money you've already spent, but didn't have to pay out for two (to three) months, to work for you in an interest bearing account.

Charge! and you not only pay with your credit cards, you make them pay off—for you.

CHAPTER III

How to Save Up to 33⅓ Percent On Credit Card Interest Charges

---

What's the best way to pay for what you buy? Here's a run-down on what it costs to pay by traveler's checks, no balance checking accounts, installments, personal loans, free checks, and even cash. How you can beat those costs with your credit cards. A check list shows you how to save whether you pay in advance, now, or later. And here's how to cut all credit card interest charges from 18 to 12 percent. Plus where to get traveler's checks free, and an idea for a traveler's check that makes money for you.

You've got to pay to pay. You can pay in advance. You can pay on the barrelhead. You can pay later. But however you pay, it costs you money *above the purchase price* to make a payment. Even when you pay with greenbacks.

What you have to do is cut the costs of those payments. It could save you hundreds of dollars a year. And you *can.* With your credit cards. Here are the guidelines to slashing the costs of paying, no matter how you feel you have to pay.

*   *   *

IF YOU FEEL YOU HAVE TO PAY IN ADVANCE

"Pay in advance? That's a ridiculous thought," an experienced woman shopper told us bitterly. "With services getting worse and goods getting shoddier every day, who'd want to pay in advance? Why do you think I use credit cards and charge accounts? Before I pay a cent I want to be sure I'm not stuck with a lemon and I'm getting every bit of value I'm paying for." Yet millions of Americans put up billions of dollars for goods and services *in advance*. They do it when they buy traveler's checks.

Isn't that what a traveler's check is; a payment in advance? You pay *now* for goods and services you're not going to purchase for weeks, months, and sometimes years. Most banks charge $2 for every $100 of traveler's checks. American Express charges only $1. Three thousand dollars worth of checks can cost you anywhere from $30 to $60.

What you buy with your money is safety. When you purchase your checks, you sign them in the presence of the teller. When you make payments with your checks, you sign them again in the presence of the seller. If the signatures match, your traveler's checks are accepted like cash. Forgery is required to misuse your checks. Besides, you couldn't care less if they are misused or not. You lose nothing. The moment you report your checks as lost or stolen, the bank or company that issued the checks will replace them. (*Warning:* You'll have no trouble getting replacements if you've kept the receipt you get when your checks are issued. It bears the serial numbers of the checks. Present the receipt, and you'll get fast action. Without the receipt though, you may be without money for several days. Also, even with the receipt, you can go moneyless if your loss occurred on weekends or holidays. You'll have to wait for regular business hours for the offices to open. Also: Be sure you know which of your checks had already been used by you before the balance was stolen. If you're not sure, you can be in for delays.)

But safety isn't all that you buy when you pay for your traveler's checks. You also get:

INSTANT MONEY in virtually all the currencies of the world. Your traveler's checks, made out in dollars (American) is changed on sight to francs in France, lira in Italy, pound sterling in England, pesos in Mexico, and so on. We've traveled globally and we've never had any trouble changing our traveler's checks into the coin of the realm, except in one place. The bank where we bought them in the first place. You also get:

A PREFERENTIAL RATE OF EXCHANGE. Which means that if you're in a foreign country, your dollar can be exchanged for so-and-so many francs, lira, pound sterling, pesos, and so on. But if you convert your traveler's checks at the foreign offices of the issuing bank or company, you'll get *more* francs, lira, pound sterling, pesos and so on for your dollar than you'll get anyplace else. You'll even get more than you will for greenbacks. (*Hint:* Never pay for purchases with traveler's checks. The rate of exchange is lowest in shops and restaurants, and not much higher even at the better hotels. Instead, go to the local offices of the bank or company that issued your checks, convert them into local currency [remember: This is the highest rate of exchange you can get], and pay for everything with cash. For safety's sake draw only enough cash to last you for a few days. You may save enough money this way for an extra night at Maxim's.)

So it seems that paying the $2 for $100 worth of traveler's checks is a worthwhile investment. *Not* if you can get traveler's checks for less. And you can. You can buy $5,000 worth of checks for only $2. That's only 4¢ for $100 worth of checks. You can get this bargain in the late Winter or early Spring when banks put their traveler's checks on *sale.* And you can get traveler's checks *for nothing,* anytime, at Barclay's Bank. Barclay's is a London based financial empire bigger than Bank America and First National City Bank put together. You'll find Barclay branches all over the world; in this country: in New York, in California, and importantly, at New York's Kennedy International Airport. So if you must use traveler's checks, buy them for less or, better still, if you're near a Barclay's branch, buy them for nothing.

BUT EVEN FOR NOTHING, YOU PAY DEARLY FOR TRAVELER'S CHECKS. Reason: you're tying up your money until you use those checks. That may not be for weeks, months, even years. During all that time, your money is not earning a penny for you. Example: Suppose you obtained $2,000 worth of traveler's checks at Barclay's in July and used them in August. In that month, your $2,000 could have earned you $8 or so in a savings account. The checks weren't free. You were actually paying for them at the rate of 5 percent per year.

Look what it really costs you when you take advantage of a traveler's check sale. You buy $2,000 worth of traveler's checks in May. That costs you $2. (Sale prices are ordinarily $2 for any amount up to $5,000.) You don't use your checks until August. That's three months. In that time, the $2,000 in your savings account could have netted you about $25. It isn't just $2 that the $2,000 in traveler's checks cost you; it's $2 plus $25. Buy $5,000 in sale checks, and it will cost you not $2 but $2 plus about $67 in lost interest.

An even worse traveler's check booby-trap: left-overs. If you're like most travelers, you come back home with hundreds, or even thousands of dollars in traveler's checks left-over. You don't want to cash them in, because you know you're going to travel again. Why pay for them twice? So you hold on to them for another year. And if your plans are deferred, another year. And another year. One of our friends hung on to about $400 in traveler's checks for eight years. He lost almost $200 in savings bank interest on it. The $400 tied up in checks dropped in value because of eight years of inflation. Instead of having $200 more, he ended up with *less than* the $400 he'd come home with, measured in the buying power of the dollar eight years later. *Advice:* If you have leftover traveler's checks, deposit them at once in your savings account. You'll need those extra interest dollars to make up for the loss in value of the dollars you have due to inflation.

Traveler's checks add to the cost of the things you buy with them. Here's an example: Had you waited until a month before you planned to use the checks, and bought them at your bank after the sale was over, say at $2 per $100, the cost for $2,000 worth of checks would be (two times 20 hundreds) $40, *plus* about $8 in lost savings account interest, for a total of $48. That means you'd be paying ($48 divided by $2,000) almost 2½ percent more on everything you'd buy with those checks.

*   *   *

Once you know the real cost of traveler's checks, it hurts. But what hurts even more is something else the banks have concealed from you. Read these facts and weep.

Banks use the money you deposit with them to make money—by means of loans, investments and other financial transactions—*for themselves.* That's why they're willing to pay you interest. They're really buying the use of your money at 5 percent, so they can put it to work to net them 10 to 20 percent. The principle is fair enough, even though the ratio of what *you* get and what the *banks* get from your money is out of whack; they earn more than 400 percent more than you do on *your* dollar. You should get *more* interest. But when you put your money in traveler's checks, you get no interest at all. Worse, *you* pay the bank.

To spell this out: What you do, in essence, when you buy bank traveler's checks is to transfer funds from your savings account, on which the bank has to pay you, to your "traveler's checking account," on which you have to pay the bank (Barclay's excepted). So when you deposit your money in a "traveler's checking account," *you're actually paying the bank to use your money to make money for itself.* (You've done the same for decades in your Christmas Club account. *You've* played Santa Claus to the bank.) See why the banks don't tell you all the facts about traveler's checks?

What can you do about it? If you must use traveler's checks, you can limit the amount of time the bank has the use of your money at your expense. (And, of course, get the leftovers out of your hands and into your savings account *right now*.) But even if you buy your traveler's checks on the day you leave, you're going to be away for a week, two, or longer, and some of the money isn't going to be spent until the end of the trip. The bank has the use of your money until then. The use of your money even for a single day is of importance to a bank. Banks, for example, frequently make "overnight" loans to other banks at low interest rates, about 6 to 10 percent. If they had to pay you 5 percent for that money, their profit margin would be small; but when they can use your traveler's check money free of charge, loans of this type bring in a sizeable profit. No matter how carefully you use your traveler's checks, you're giving the bank free money, and the bank makes money on it.

The banks would like to have more of this free money. That's the reason for traveler's check sales. That's probably the reason Barclay's puts no charge on its traveler's checks. Fact is, the small amount of money you pay for your traveler's checks is of no importance to the banks. What they want is your traveler's check money. If the banks were certain that giving you the traveler's checks for nothing would induce you to put more of your money into their no-interest "traveler's checking accounts," they'd give them to you for nothing. But marketing experts point out that if they were offered free, the public would be suspicious and the volume of traveler's checks issued would drop. (Apparently, the Barclay experience has done nothing to alter this opinion. And, as a matter of fact, we understand that Barclay's in New York is under great pressure from the banking industry to cease issuing free traveler's checks.) But even a more important drawback to the issuance of free traveler's checks, according to these sales specialists, is the embarrassing question which would certainly arise. "Nobody gives something for nothing; how come?" To which the banks would have to answer. An honest answer would do nothing to endear the banks to the public. It would be: "We need your money. But we don't want to pay you for it."

We feel that if the banks need your money, they should pay for it. So why not replace the traveler's check that you pay for with:

A TRAVELER'S CHECK
THAT PAYS *YOU.*

Here's how it works:

Background: a recap of two well-known facts about savings accounts.

One. There's nothing new about banks and Savings and Loan Associations offering daily interest. That is, interest from date of deposit to date of withdrawal. Usually, it's offered with passbook accounts, but it is also offered with *savings certificates.*

Two. For years now, you've been able to pay off a debt by sending your passbook to your bank with instructions to

withdraw a certain amount from your account in the form
of a check to your creditor. Your passbook and the savings
account check is then returned to you. (You can get the check
in person as well as by mail.)

Action:

Put those two facts together. *One,* a daily interest bearing
savings certificate. *Two,* a savings account check. *One* plus
two, a daily interest bearing savings certificate that's also a
check. If the check isn't made out to anybody in particular,
but is signed by you in the presence of the teller, and it must
be signed by you again (countersigned) in the presence of
the seller before it is acceptable, then it becomes a traveler's
check. *A daily interest bearing traveler's check. The traveler's check that pays you.*

In every other respect, including issuance in a variety of
denominations and all the security and convenience features,
the traveler's check that pays you is the same as the traveler's check for which you pay. With this kind of traveler's
check, the longer you hold it, the more it's worth. If our
friend, who held on to his $400 worth of leftovers for eight
years, had been holding an interest bearing traveler's check,
he would have gained $200 instead of losing it. The amount
of interest you earn from the date of issuance is calculated
for you, and set up in an easy-to-read chart on the check, so
you always know how much the check is worth. Hold this
new kind of traveler's check for $400 long enough, and you
can pay off a $600 bill with it.

One drawback to *the traveler's check that pays you;*
it doesn't exist. Yet. It's our idea, and we offer it to
the banking industry. With it, the banking industry could
minimize the competition from non-banking type traveler's checks. This would be a gain for the banks because

they would be getting *more* money with which to operate. ("Money is the life blood of all banks," asserts a spokesman for the Franklin State Bank of New Brunswick, N. J. "Money makes money which gives us more money to make money with. Our bank loves you. For your money.") You'd gain too, because at long last, you'd be getting paid for the money on which the banks make money. *The traveler's check that pays you,* in any variety, is inevitable, once more and more of the public know the true facts about traveler's checks as we've brought them to you, and refuse to buy traveler's checks as they exist now—even for nothing.

That means there must be alternatives to the traveler's check. There are. Remember that what the traveler's check gives you is protection against loss, universal acceptability, instant local currency, and a preferential rate of exchange. A personal check is as safe as a traveler's check. (If you lose your checkbook, you can always use blanks, except for some special checking accounts.) When a personal check is backed up by a bank guarantee card (the bank pays off if you can't pay up), you can use it for purchases almost anywhere, and convert it into foreign currency at any foreign bank. If you convert it at a foreign branch of your own bank, where the chances are you'll get better exchange rates than at other banks, you won't get as much local currency for your dollar as you would with your bank's traveler's checks, but the difference will be slight.

Watch out though: Checks also cost you money. If you deposit $2,000 in your checking account to cover travel expenses, you're losing the interest you'd be earning if that money were in your savings account. Same situation as you were in with your traveler's checks. If you're thinking of getting around this situation by keeping that $2,000 in your savings account, but writing checks for $2,000 on your "checking plus" account which permits you to spend in excess of your balance—*don't*. While your $2,000 in your savings account will be earning at the rate of 5 percent per year, the $2,000 you spend will cost you 12 to 18 percent per year. You can end up worse off than if you'd bought traveler's checks.

Another warning: If you don't have a bank guarantee card, you'll find that passing a personal check will be extremely difficult.

But you'll have no trouble at all passing your credit cards. *No matter what part of the world you're in, they're your passport to money. Credit cards can be used in place of traveler's checks.* One brilliant TV commercial has a bored-with-it-all executive walk out of his job in the midst of a sales meeting, and wing off to faraway places with strange sounding names, without cash, luggage or airline tickets, changing the "can-you-pay?" frowns of hotel managers and shop owners into beaming welcomes when he flashes his credit card. You can travel around the globe funded *only* with credit cards. You can buy anything you need at more than half a million outlets, stay at the best hotels, pick up at least $50 in local currency in all the major cities, book transportation. In that TV commercial the executive floats off into the China Seas on a sampan —passage paid for by his credit card.

And, of course, when you use your credit cards, you *make* money. Use the same four card method abroad as you learned how to use here (see Chapter II), and you'll find that your *Real* Charge Date can be as much as a month removed from the date you made your charge. You'll be able to get as much as three months of free credit on your bank cards and four months on your T&E cards. Ever make money with the money you spend on vacation? You can—with credit cards. And it's more money than you'll make with your cards when you're at work back home. Here, the most free credit time you can get is two or three months. The extra month that you can get from charging abroad lets your money work that much longer for you in your savings account.

But be careful. If you lose your credit card, or if it's stolen, it's not readily replaceable while you're abroad. You're liable for all amounts charged up on it after it's left your possession until you report the loss. And reporting the loss might not be easy if you're in a small hamlet outside of Bangkok.

Should you pay in advance with traveler's checks? If you want to buy safety, and you don't have a bank check guarantee, the answer is *yes*. But if you want to take the chances of loss or theft, go along with your credit cards. You not only don't pay in advance—you don't pay for months. And all that time, the money you're spending is earning money for you. Until *the traveler's check that pays you* becomes a reality, the credit card is your best bet. With it, you can make your vacation with pay—pay more.

*　　*　　*

IF YOU FEEL YOU HAVE TO PAY ON THE BARRELHEAD

You think: "I've got the money in my checking account. It's not earning me anything anyway. What's the difference if I pay now or pay later? Besides, I've got one of those free checking accounts. The check doesn't cost me anything. I might as well pay now and get it over with."

But the truth is, your "free" checking account is far from free. As a matter of fact, it's very frequently more costly than a "special checking account" with its monthly maintenance charge and a fee for each check. Follow your dollar through a free checking account and a special checking account at the Chase Manhattan Bank, and you'll see why.

Here are the costs of the two kinds of accounts reproduced from Chase's promotion literature:

CHASE PERSONAL CHECKING ACCOUNTS

ACTIVITY PLAN
(Special)

Monthly maintenance charge	$.75
Each check paid—as listed on monthly statement . . .	.10

BALANCE PLAN
(Regular)

Average balance	Monthly Fee	Charge Per Check
$500. or more	Free	None
$400. — $499.	$1.	None
$300. — $399.	$2.	None
$200. — $299.	$3.	None
0 — $199.	$4.	None

Note the ground rules: The special checking account, Chase's *Activity Plan,* costs you 75¢ a month plus 10¢ a check. The free checking account, Chase's regular checking account, renamed the *Balance Plan,* is free only when your average balance is at least $500. That's the joker. That $500 isn't earning you a penny, whereas in your savings account it would earn at the rate of 5 percent per year. That's ($500 times 5%) $25 a year, which is the cost of getting your checking account free. And that's a minimum cost. The higher your average monthly balance, the greater the cost. Keep $600 in your account, just to be on the safe side (you don't want to slip to $499 and pay a penalty), and you're paying $30 a year.

If you do slip below the minimum, the costs really begin to mount. Slip just one buck under $500, and you have to pay a buck. The lower you slip, the more it costs. Reach the lower depths of $199 or less, and you add $4 to your monthly expenses. Now, and this is the important point, the extra cost is slapped on your account on the basis of your average balance *during* a month. You might have had an average balance of $4,000 last month, but if it sinks to $199 this month, your average for two months is well over $500, but you'll still be penalized four bucks. Carry out this situation over twelve months and you can run up a sizeable bill for "free" checking.

Here's how it figures out. One month's average balance: $4,000. The average balance for each of the other 11 months: $199. Average monthly balance for the year, $4,000 plus $199 times 11 months all divided by 12 months, equals a bit more than $515. Above the minimum. But you'll still be charged $4 a month for the 11 months at $199. That's $44. However, with an *annual* average balance of $500 a month, a daily interest savings account will pay $25 interest for the year ($500 times 5%) no matter how much the *monthly* average balance might fluctuate. So your cost for "free" checking under these circumstances, could be $69 ($25 plus $44) a year.

For $25 to $69 a year, which is the lower and upper range of costs for free checking on an average yearly balance of $500 per month, you can write an unlimited amount of checks. If you write a thousand checks per year, your cost comes down to a maximum of only 6.9¢ per check. But you don't write a thousand checks a year, and you certainly don't write an unlimited number of checks. If you're like most Americans, you'll be writing less than 150 checks per year, which means your free checks will cost you between 17¢ ($25 divided by 150 checks) and 46¢ per check ($69 divided by 150 checks).

On the other hand, checks that are supposed to cost you more, "special checking account" checks, actually cost you less. Since no minimum balance is required, you can keep a monthly average balance of a buck so you're not losing interest on $500 each month. Your only charges are 75¢ per month maintenance fee; that's $9 a year, and 10¢ a check for 150 checks; that's $15 a year. Total yearly cost $24 ($9 plus $15). And that makes the cost of a single check only 16¢ ($24 divided by 150 checks). Compare that with the cost of 17¢ to 46¢ for a "free" check.

The brutal fact is, unless you're writing more than 150 checks a year, you're paying more for your "free"' checks than you are for your 10¢ apiece checks. If you want to determine whether it's wiser for you to use a "free" checking account or a "special," estimate the number of checks you'll write this year based on the number you wrote last year (just count them up from last year's records), then use the chart on the opposite page.

Here are some astonishing facts revealed by the chart. If you write only 25 checks a year and keep a monthly average balance of $150, you pay as much as $2.22 for each "free" check. Sustain the minimum balance of $500, and each of those 25 "free" checks still cost you $1.00. On a special checking account, writing the same number of checks a year (25), the cost per check is only 46¢. On the other hand, once you write more than 150 checks a year, you're better off with "free" checks, provided you keep your monthly average balance at $500. When your average balance falls as low as $150, you'll have to write more than 500 checks a year before the cost per "free" check is less than the cost of the special check.

HOW TO DETERMINE WHEN 'FREE' CHECKS COST MORE THAN CHECKS THAT COST MONEY

Number of checks per year	Maximum cost of a "free" check with average monthly balances of					Cost of a "special" check—no minimum balance required
	$600	$500	$450	$250	$150	
25	$1.20	$1.00	$1.38	$1.94	$2.22	$ .46
50	.60	.50	.69	.97	1.11	.29
75	.40	.33	.46	.65	.74	.22
100	.30	.25	.35	.49	.56	.19
125	.24	.20	.28	.39	.44	.17
150	.20	(.17)	.23	.32	.37	(.16)
200	.15	.13	.17	.24	.28	.15
250	.12	.10	.14	.19	.22	.14
300	.10	.08	.12	.16	.19	.13
400	.08	.06	.09	.12	.14	.12
500	.06	.05	.07	.10	.11	.12
600	.05	.04	.06	.08	.09	.12

'Special' Checks Are Cheaper ←

'Free' Checks Are Cheaper →

Calculations are based on loss of daily interest at 5 percent and penalties assessed for failing to sustain balance of $500 (monthly average). Costs are "minimum" since it is assumed in the $500 and $600 columns that this balance is sustained each month. If not, as explained in the text, costs could go up 400 percent or more. Chart based on costs established by Chase Manhattan Bank (see page 48).

There's one kind of check that doesn't cost you money. It's the savings account check, and most banks will let you have a number of them without charge. They're truly free because your money *is* in a savings account drawing interest, so you're not losing money as if your funds were tied up in a checking account. However, when you pay on the barrelhead with a savings account check, you're making the same mistake as if you'd paid with greenbacks. The mistake is not using your credit card instead. Remember with your credit cards (using the four card method), you can get two or three months free credit anytime during the month (see Chapter II). For up to three months the money you've already spent could be earning interest for you. *It costs you money when you pay with cash* whether it's with regular checks, special checks, or even with free savings account checks or greenbacks.

It all adds up to this: *Don't* pay on the barrelhead. Pay by credit card instead. Then when you have to pay, pay with the least costly kind of check, usually a savings account check. (Except if you're in Watertown, Massachusetts. The Coolidge Bank and Trust Company there provides free checking account checks with *no* minimum balance required. You may find similar offers made by some 200 smalltown banks nationwide.) However, *if you can get a discount by paying on the barrelhead, pay.* You can check if *that* kind of deal is to your advantage.

*   *   *

IF YOU FEEL YOU HAVE TO PAY LATER

There are three general ways you can go about doing it. One, you can buy on installments. Two, you can borrow the cash, then pay back the cash. Three, you can pay with your credit cards. Which way is the least expensive for you?

INSTALLMENTS. Until bank credit cards deluged the populace, installment buying was the standard means of buying on time. It's still around, called by various names like time-purchase agreement, retail installment contract, or conditional sales contract. See page 54 for a sample of a typical contract of this type:

You'll note (lower left hand corner) that the acceptance signature is *printed* in, not written in. That's because, despite the warning that it's "Accepted (Subject to Credit Approval)", credit approval is almost a certainty unless you're an established deadbeat. The reason: See the line of small print just above the "DESCRIPTION OF GOODS AND/OR SERVICES." It reads: "The Buyer agrees that title to the goods shall remain in the Seller until they are fully paid for." Translation: The store owns whatever you bought—you *don't* own it—until you've made your final payment. Unless you pay every last cent of the list price *plus* the price of accessories, *plus* the sales tax, *plus* the excise tax, *plus* the finance charges, *plus* the delinquency charges, *plus* the collection charges, the merchant can take back the goods—and resell the goods according to law. If you get back any of the money, you can consider yourself one of the lucky ones. The merchant is therefore willing to extend credit readily, because he knows he can seize the merchandise, "repossess" it, if you default. Buying by installments is dangerous if, for any reason at all, you can't pay up.

What's more, you're trapped by these contracts even though you may have valid reasons for not paying. For example: You buy a refrigerator, but it doesn't work. You complain to the merchant you bought it from. He tells you he's sold your installment contract to a finance company. He's sorry the refrigerator doesn't work, but he's out of the picture. That's true. So you go to the finance company and repeat your complaint. The executives tell you they're shocked to hear

RETAIL INSTALLMENT CONTRACT
(Conditional Sales Contract)

To: **R. H. MACY & CO., INC.** (The Seller)

Each person who appears as a Buyer at the foot hereof separately agrees with the Seller to purchase and pay for goods and/or services as hereinafter provided. The Buyer agrees that title to the goods shall remain in the Seller until they are fully paid for.

. . . .

Finance Charge begins to accrue on date of delivery of goods. The Total of Payments shall be payable in _____ consecutive monthly installments of

$ _____ each and a final installment of $ _____ beginning on the first monthly billing date after delivery, and on the corresponding date of each month thereafter.

Upon default in payment of any installment due hereunder for a period of 10 days, Seller may impose a delinquency charge of 5% of such installment, or **$5.00**, whichever is less, and at Seller's option all amounts then remaining unpaid shall become immediately due and payable.

An extension of time granted to the Buyer for payment of any sum which may become due the Seller hereunder shall not relieve the Buyer of obligation to pay subsequent amounts promptly when due.

If the Buyer prepays the full amount due, he shall be entitled to a refund of any unearned portion of the Finance Charge (if more than **$1.00**) based upon the rule of 78's.

NOTICE TO THE BUYER:

1. Do not sign this agreement before you read it or if it contains any blank space.

2. You are entitled to a completely filled in copy of this agreement.

3. Under the law, you have the right to pay off in advance the full amount due and under certain conditions to obtain a partial refund of the Finance Charge.

Accepted (Subject to Credit Approval)

Seller:
R. H. MACY & CO., INC.
Herald Square
New York, N.Y. 10001

By _____
Assistant Treasurer, Macy's, New York

F. 3462K   6-69

I hereby acknowledge receipt of an executed copy of this RETAIL INSTALLMENT CONTRACT.

Buyer(s) _____   Date _____

_____
(Buyer's Signature)

_____
(Address)

City _____   State _____   Zip Code _____

that the merchant sold you a faulty refrigerator, but how could they know? They're innocent, and you wouldn't want innocent people to pay for something somebody else did, would you?

Even if you would, you couldn't. The law sees the finance company as an "innocent third party," and you have no legal claim against them. Your only course of action is to withhold payment. But when you do, the finance company invokes the conditions of the contract and *without notice* garnishees your salary and repossesses its merchandise. *And* hits you with staggering legal fees and penalties to which you had agreed *in advance* when you signed the contract. There's not a thing you can do. (In some states, pending remedial legislation will force the finance companies and other holders of installment contracts *to give notice* before repossessing or garnisheeing, and in one state the purchaser has been given the right to a trial *before* the contract owners can garnishee or repossess.)

What's it cost to run this financial obstacle course? Finance charges of 16.5 percent per year are normal for reputable outfits. That's cheaper than the 18 percent you'll have to pay normally on most credit card purchases. But that 16.5 percent is booby trapped. If you're more than 10 days late on any installment (even if you've been paying all the other installments on time, or before they were due), you can be slapped with a delinquency charge of 5 percent on that installment. On a $100 installment, you'll have to pay $5 more. That means you're paying additional interest at the rate of 60 percent per year.

However, installment buying with all its built-in hazards can be cheaper than—

PERSONAL LOANS. A personal bank loan costs you, on the average, 18 percent per year. Finance companies charge you about 24 percent per year. One Kentucky finance company's annual lending rate, authorized by state law, is 38.25 percent.

If you're making a personal loan, therefore, your best bet is your bank. Not only because the loan costs you less, but because you can borrow more money than at a finance company. The highest amount that you can get from that Kentucky finance company is $800. Tops from other finance companies is about $1,400. How much more you can get from a bank depends on your income, your bank balance, and of course, your credit-ability. If your credit-ability, that is to say, your proven ability to pay off credit in the past, and your current ability to pay off credit out of your income is good, then you can determine how much you can raise from a bank by a simple rule of thumb. It's this: Divide your average monthly bank balance by three. If the money in your savings account *and* in your checking account adds up to a monthly total of $6,000 (for at least a year), your bank is likely to let you have $2,000. Actually, though, the bank can lend you any amount it chooses, subject to state law, and you'll have to work out the amount of your loan when you sit down with your bank's loan officer. Few personal loans though exceed $25,000. This is why that's the maximum amount covered by the Truth in Lending Law. As a matter of practice, most banks limit their personal credit ceiling to $5,000.

To combat these advantages of the banks, finance companies stress that "it's *easier* for you to get the money you need *here*." It's a valid claim. We know of a man who, turned down by several banks for a $400 loan to meet pressing medical needs (his credit-ability *was* bad), obtained the money overnight from a finance company on his signature and the collateral of his household furniture. Because of the larger return on their investments, finance companies are willing to take larger risks. One Kentucky company will let you have up to $800 *by mail.* "You don't have to see anyone," the company promises. "There is no security or collateral required . . . no co-signers are needed . . . no one will call on you . . . and no wage assignments [garnishments] are taken. This is the dignified, businesslike way to take care of your personal financial matters." But on an $800 loan, you get only $778.38 in cash, and the finance charges paid back over 30 months comes to $374.52. You get $778.38 and you pay back $1,152.90!

Fact is, that while it *is* easier to get a loan at a finance company, the banks are making it easier and easier for you to come to them for your personal finances. Major hurdle to most bank loan applicants in the past was the loan application interview. In the tradition of old-fashioned banking, it was reminiscent of a schoolboy's visit to the principal's office. Today, loans by mail and dial-a-loans are lifting applicants lightly over the interview hurdle. Even the application itself is eliminated when you apply for another loan after the first loan has been granted. "You apply just once," according to the First National City Bank, "and depending on your ability to repay, we set up a cash reserve for you—from $400 to $5,000. Forget about it until you need it. Then write a check bigger than your balance. We automatically loan you the money to cover it. Instantly. No trips to the bank. No phone calls. No applications. As you pay, the reserve builds up. So you can use it again and again." You simply write yourself a loan.

If you feel you must pay cash for what you buy, and you haven't got the cash, and you can meet bank credit-ability standards (careful: a bank official told us that only one out of three Americans can), then get the money from your bank. It's not the traumatic experience it used to be and it *is* the cheapest way you can make a personal loan.

But it's not the cheapest way to make purchases. Interest on your bank loan begins the day the money is credited to your account. But with a bank credit card, interest need not begin (see Chapter II) for two months. That cuts your cost. What's more, interest on personal bank loans are often set at 18 percent per year no matter what the size of the loan, but on credit card purchases interest is 18 percent only for the first $500; it drops to 12 percent on the balance over $500. And that cuts your cost. There's even a way to cut your costs further when you use your credit cards.

YOU CAN CUT THE COST OF CREDIT CARD PURCHASES FROM 18 PERCENT TO 12 PERCENT

The method is based on this little known (and never publicized) fact about the two major bank credit cards. When you charge goods and services on either of these two cards, you pay the normal 18 percent per year for the first $500 of unpaid balance. But, *when you charge cash advances,* you pay only 12.17 percent per year with your (First National City Bank's) *Master Charge, and only 12 percent per year with your* (Bankers Trust Company's) *BankAmericard.* That's a savings of 33⅓ percent.*

What you have to do to slash your 18 percent per year cost of extended credit to as low as 12 percent is this. When your bank credit card bill for goods and services comes due (that is: on the payment date), charge cash advances with your bank credit card for the amount of the bill. Pay the bill with the advance. Then pay the installments when due, *not* at 18 percent, but at 12 percent.

_____

Each bank issuing either of the major plans' cards sets its own interest rate—usually the maximum permitted under its state law.

Example: You've charged up $200 in goods and services with your BankAmericard. When that $200 is due, charge a cash advance of $200 with the same or other card. Pay off your bill with the $200. Then pay off the installments on the $200 at 12 percent per year, *not* 18 percent.

You see the advantage of charging an advance on *the due date* not on *the purchase date*. If you charged the advance on the purchase date and paid in cash, you'd be paying interest *from the date of purchase*. But by charging with your credit card, interest doesn't begin until the due date, which could be as much as two months later. You save two months interest charges.

Hint: If one card doesn't give you enough cash to cover your bill, use two. Example: You've run up charges of $400 in goods and services on your BankAmericard and your credit limit is $500. Raise $100 on your BankAmericard and $300 on your Master Charge card.

It all adds up to this: when you pay later, the cheapest way to pay is with your credit card, particularly when you cut the cost of credit card interest by a whopping third, and take advantage of the months of free credit that you can get.

And remember: No matter if you pay in advance, or on the barrelhead, or later, if you can get a discount with cash, take the discount. And final hint: If you don't have the cash, then take a cash advance on your bank credit card (1 percent per month interest)—*provided* you get a large enough discount to make it worthwhile.

*   *   *

Whether you pay in advance, now, or later, you have a choice of the way you pay. Here's a check list which shows you how to save when you make that choice.

IF YOU FEEL YOU HAVE TO PAY IN
ADVANCE, USE:

☐ Barclay's free traveler's checks, which give you safety but lose you earnings on the money you've tied up.

☐ Other traveler's checks, which also give you safety and lose you money, but which charge you a premium as well.

Or

☐ Don't pay in advance, but use your credit cards and charge as you go. Watch the money you spend make money for you.

IF YOU FEEL YOU HAVE TO PAY ON THE
BARRELHEAD, USE:

☐ Cash, or the equivalent in savings account checks, which lose you earnings on the money you spend.

☐ Special checks, which cost you additional money.

☐ Free checks, which can be more expensive.

Or

☐ Don't pay on the barrelhead, but use your credit cards to push back due dates for two to three months. Let your money earn money for you in your savings account during that time.

IF YOU FEEL YOU HAVE TO PAY LATER, USE:

☐ Installment credit. This can cost you 16.5 percent per year minimum, but if you don't pay because of faulty merchandise or any other reason, you may lose the merchandise *and* every cent you paid before you stopped payments.

☐ Personal loans from finance companies, which cost you from 24 to nearly 40 percent per year.

☐ Personal loans from banks, or the equivalent bank check credit advances, which cost you 18 percent per year.

Or

☐ Don't use any credit except your credit cards. Get months of free credit, then pay off your bills for goods and services with credit card cash advances and save 33⅓ percent on interest charges.

CHAPTER IV

How to Get Discounts—
Just by Waiving
Your Credit Card

---

*You know who foots the bill for your retailers'
credit card service?* You. *Through higher prices.
The credit card takes a bite out of your
pocketbook everytime you make a purchase*—even
though you pay in cash. *Here's how to take the
teeth out of "credit card bite" and obtain sizeable
reductions of prices. And here's a new kind of card
to help you do it*—the UNCREDIT CARD.

In the previous chapters, you've learned how to *make*
money with your credit card. In this chapter, you'll learn how
to *save* money by taking advantage of the credit card *system*.

This means that you'll be able to get discounts where
you've never been able to get them before. You'll do it with
a simple straightforward deal that most retailers will be eager
to accept. Here's the story:

Ask your retailer what the credit card costs him every
time you charge up a sale. He'll tell you that, on the average,
banks take 5 percent of the sales total, T&E card services
take 7 percent. (That's on the average. The "take" often goes
higher. Although "5 percent is most typical," according to
the Federal Reserve Bank of New York, *Life* magazine finds
that banks often "ask . . . merchants for . . . kickbacks to 6½
percent on all credit card transactions." Some banks grab as

much as 8 percent, and some T&E card bites exceed 10 percent.)

Ask your retailer what he does to write off these whopping kickbacks and he'll answer there's only one thing he can do; he soups up his prices. He passes the cost on to the consumer. That's you. Every time you make a purchase with a credit card, *you're* paying for his credit card service bite.

That's bad. But it's even worse when you pay with cash. Because the price is the same whether you pay with cash or you pay with your credit card. It's the same souped up credit price.

At least when you pay with a credit card, you get something in return for your extra dough; you get credit. But when you pay with cash, you don't even get that. For your extra dough, you get *nothing* in return.

So when you pay with cash, you're paying for the merchandise *and* for the credit that you're *not* getting. That's not fair, is it? You should get *a discount* for cash. You *should.* But try to get it. Just try. Leave your credit cards at home, and walk into your retailer's and say, "I'll take that, but I'm paying with cash. What's the discount?" You'll be told politely but firmly, "The price on the price tag is the price you pay. We don't have a two price policy." High credit price? Yes. Low cash price? *No!*

Obviously, your retailer doesn't see how fair your request is. So you've got to *persuade* him to give you that discount for cash that you deserve. How do you persuade him? Remember the story of the farmer who couldn't budge his mule? He dangled a carrot in front of the animal, then whacked him on his behind with a stick to force him toward the carrot. Your credit card is your carrot *and* your stick. Here's how you use it:

Go back to the retailer who turned you down. But this time, bring a credit card along. Plunk down your credit card, and say, "Charge it, *but—*" And here it comes. *"But,* I'm willing to *waive* my credit card, *not* use it, and pay cash instead. *If,* in return, you give me a discount."

Your retailer will look at the credit card, and make some fast mental calculations.

It's a bank card, so he'll figure that if he *charges* the sale, he'll have to fork over 5 percent of the selling price to the bank. But if he *doesn't* charge the sale, if he takes *cash* instead, he won't have to give the bank a cent. He'll have 5 percent of the selling price to play with. He can give *you* 4 percent as a discount and keep 1 percent *for himself.*

See why your credit card is a carrot?

Now for the stick.

"But if you don't want to give me a discount," you tell him, "why you go right ahead and charge it." So instead of putting 1 percent of the sale in his pocket, he'll have to hand out 5 percent to the bank. *Whack!*

Think he'll be persuaded?

Here's what happened to people like yourself when they tried it.

A businessman we know bought two suits. The bill came to about $350. He shoved a bank credit card across the counter. "Tell you what I'll do," he told the proprietor, "knock something off that price, and I'll pay cash."

"Fifteen bucks enough?" the proprietor shot back.

It was enough. The businessman saved more than 4 percent.

Here's another case.

A young woman who lives in Manhattan's Greenwich Village bought a lamp in a local boutique. She handed over her T&E credit card; then almost as an afterthought, said, "Gee, could I get it a little cheaper if I paid for cash?"

"Sure can," the manager answered without giving it any thought at all. "How about we just wipe out as much as the sales tax?"

In New York City the sales tax is 6 percent—and that's how much she saved. (Remember: on T&E cards, the average credit card company bite is higher than the banks', 7 percent as opposed to 5, so you can expect bigger discounts with T&E cards.)

Notice that she didn't have to spell out the deal, and neither did the businessman. Once you plop your credit card on the counter and ask for a discount with cash, your retailer understands. He's lived with the hard facts of credit card economics long enough. He can see the carrot and feel the stick, without your calling his attention to them. Given the choice between selling at full price on a credit card, or at a lower price for cash, he knows that he'll make more when he sells for less—for cash.

In addition, your retailer often has three other reasons for accepting your deal.

One: The discount buys your good will. You'll come back. You'll refer your friends. "Why don't you try my retailer? He'll give you a discount." You're likely to use the money you save to, as one retailer put it, "Buy more at my store."

Two: Many T&E credit card companies take their own sweet time to pay him for the purchases you make on their credit cards. Your retailer would much rather have your cash today than wait 30, 60, 90 days or longer for their checks. "Banks credit your account sometimes the same day," another retailer commented, "but I still prefer cash. You know, the stuff that goes over the counter, not numbers on a ledger that anybody can audit, like the IRS. You can get away with a lot more with cash, if you know what I mean."

And three: The credit card service charge levied on the retailer has stirred up deep resentment. One retailer complained to us, "In the old days the Mafia used to put the muscle on us for a 5, 10 percent bite. Now it's the banks and the credit cards companies. But what's the difference? I have to put up or go out of business." One of New York's finest restaurants, now has to put this notice on each of its tables:

> **We would greatly appreciate it if you would pay the waiter's tip in cash since credit plans have extended their commission charges to all items including tips.
> Receipt available.**
>
> **Thank You**

Reduced from original size.

The proprietor explains: "I have to pay my waiters the full amount of the tips. But the credit card services don't give me the full amount back. They take a bite of the tips. It costs me 5 percent, more, everytime somebody charges a tip. I'm sorry I ever got into this thing in the first place." We know of one record store owner who is so incensed by the credit card bite that he offers discounts as high as 10 percent when you pay with cash instead of using a credit card. One Long Island (New York) lingerie shop, known for its discounts, bites back by greeting its customers at the cash register with

"10 percent off for cash, 5 percent off for charge." Most retailers welcome the opportunity to beat the bite.

So persuasive is the total force of all these reasons that some retailers will actually give you discounts even on a clearance sale price when you waive your credit card. If your experience is like most Americans, you know that never before were you able to get discounts at such sales, anywhere at any time. But I know you can do it now, because I did it.

At the end of a summer clearance sale, I stopped into one of New York's posh shoe stores and selected two pairs of shoes. Pre-sale price $42 a pair. Sale price: under $20. "Fabulous bargain," the salesman explained. "Actually cost us more. But there's a new line coming in and we've got to get rid of them. Charge or cash?"

That was the first time I had heard any of this store's sales personnel mention "charge." One of the "better" shops in town, this store had turned up its nose at credit cards for years. Even now, the salesman told me, his store accepted only one card, the most prestigious of the T&E cards. "Charge," I said, and I fumbled through my wallet to find my card. It wasn't there. "Sorry," I said to the salesman, "must have left it in my other wallet. Put the shoes aside for me and I'll come back tomorrow."

His face fell. "Well all right," I said. "I'll pay cash now. But listen; when I charge with that card, it costs your store 7 percent, and the chances are your bookkeeper won't get a cent from the T&E people for two to three months. I'll pay cash if you knock off the amount of the sales tax, 6 percent."

The salesman said, "Number one, you're a hundred percent right about the kickback and how long it takes for us to get paid. Number two, if you leave, I'd be a lucky man if you come back tomorrow. Once a customer goes, he goes. If that happened, the store wouldn't have the cash for those shoes, and I wouldn't get the commission. Let me check with the boss."

The salesman was back in 10 seconds with the O.K., and I saved over two bucks, which I promptly invested in a pair of sox which were also on sale in the store. At 6 percent discount for cash, of course.

The point is, you don't have to "sell" the cash discount deal based on waiving your credit card. It sells itself. All *you've* got to do is *offer* it. Don't restrict yourself to retail stores. Offer it in hotels, motels, restaurants, service stations— wherever you see the credit card decals displayed. Says Andy Spanogle, Ralph Nader's consumer credit specialist, "I know that when I pull into gas stations and first offer to pay with a credit card and then offer cash, the owner is willing to give me a cent or two off per gallon rather than let me use the card."

And don't think the deal isn't worth the bother because the discounts on each purchase tend to be small, like pennies on gasoline or a pair of sox. But it's $3 when you dine out in style, and $6 for that stay in a motel. You can save as much as $25 on a hi-fi, and when you add up all your savings over a year, *it adds up*. We know of a housewife who bought a color TV, a secretary who financed a Caribbean cruise, and a student who was able to pay for a trip to a rock festival, just by waiving their credit cards.

*   *   *

Credit card wise buyers are getting cash discounts each day by offering this *credit card or cash discount* deal when it comes time to pay for goods or services. They use variants of the approaches you've just read about. So can you. It's easy. But to make it even easier, you can use a device introduced for the first time in this book. It's your passport to cash discounts. It's . . .

The UNCREDIT CARD

You'll find it on the end leaf at the back of the book. Examine it, and you'll see it does all the explaining for you. It tells your retailer *what* the deal is. And, on the off-chance that he won't recognize *how good* the deal is, it spells out all the advantages to him. In short, the UNCREDIT CARD tells your retailer you're willing to waive your credit card, if he'll give you a discount for cash; and tells him why he's better off choosing the cash.

Here's how to obtain discounts with your UNCREDIT CARD:

1. Deal *only* with the owner, manager, or somebody authorized to make price decisions.
2. When you're ready to pay, *charge!* Hand over your credit card, then, before he has a chance to do anything with it, slip him your UNCREDIT CARD.
3. Allow 30 seconds for the retailer to read the UNCREDIT CARD.
4. Then ask him, "How do you want to make the sale? Credit card or cash at a discount?"
5. Unless he has an ironclad policy of not giving a discount to anybody for anything, chances are he'll give you the discount.
6. Walk out of the store with the good feeling that comes with extra money in your pocket and a victory justly deserved.

But when you use the UNCREDIT CARD, be careful about a few things. Here are some *dont's* you should observe. (They also apply when you offer the deal without the UNCREDIT CARD.)

Don't waste time with salespeople who lack authority to make a price decision. When you're ready to present your UNCREDIT CARD, ask for the person in charge. (You'll find, though, that more and more salespeople, like the salesman in that posh New York shoe shop, are becoming hep to the advantages of accepting cash rather than a credit card. If you can't deal with a decision maker because he may be busy, start the ball rolling with your sales person.)

Don't present your UNCREDIT CARD without presenting your credit card. If you just present your UNCREDIT CARD, it's like walking into a store and asking for a discount for cash. You won't get it. Remember the rationale behind the deal. To get discounts, you must show your credit card, then offer *not* to use it. You must offer to waive it in favor of cash. When you do that, your retailer has the choice of refusing your offer and paying the credit service fee, or of accepting your offer, and putting some of that fee into his own pocket. Odds are, he'll accept. But when you don't show your credit card, you don't give him a chance to gain. All you're saying to him is: lower your price and lose. Repeat: he won't do it.

Don't insist on the discount the UNCREDIT CARD calls for—3½ percent. If your retailer wants to bargain, listen to reason. But don't go below a 50-50 split on what he would have had to pay his credit services. That is, if he's kicking back the average percents, don't take less than 2½ percent on bank cards, 3½ percent on T&E's. If your retailer is mulish, use the stick. Tell him you *won't* waive your credit card, you'll *use* it. In that case, all the service fee goes to the credit card company; he won't be able to pocket a cent. Chances are, he'll see the light.

Don't present a credit card that's not in good standing. Your retailer may check. A credit card on which no credit can be issued is like having no credit card at all. And without a credit card, as you've already been reminded, the UNCREDIT CARD won't work.

Don't try to use your UNCREDIT CARD to get discounts on airline, railroad or steamship tickets. Prices are fixed by law.

Don't try to use your UNCREDIT CARD in chain stores or department stores. They have their own built-in credit systems. They kickback *nothing* to outside sources for their credit services. So it's futile to offer to split their credit card service charge with them. A part of nothing is nothing.

And finally—

Don't walk out in a huff if your retailer refuses to honor your UNCREDIT CARD. If you want the merchandise, buy it. *With* a credit card. It'll serve him right.

* * *

But it seems as if the UNCREDIT CARD has one big drawback: It won't work in chain and department stores. It won't work *directly*, that's true. But you may be able to make it work *indirectly*. Here's how:

If you see something in a chain or department store that you want, don't buy it there. Buy it in a store that does honor your UNCREDIT CARD. If enough of you do this, it won't be long before the chain and department stores, which don't

honor your UNCREDIT CARD, will get the message—
lower prices for cash, or else.

If you want to be *sure* they get the message, why not write
a letter, and have everybody you know write letters like the
following, to the managers of your chain and department
stores, enclosing a photostat of your UNCREDIT CARD:

> Dear Sir,
>   Yesterday, I bought a television set at Mark's
> TV Shop. The price tag read $199.95, the same as
> the price tag in your store for the same item.
>   I gave the manager at Mark's TV the choice as
> shown on the enclosed photostat of my UNCREDIT
> CARD: Either he could write up the sale on my
> credit card, or give me a 3½ percent discount for
> cash.
>   He gave me the 3½ percent discount. I saved
> nearly $7.00.
>   I've told all my friends about it—and they're
> going to deal with Mark's TV, too. And with other
> merchants who give a discount for cash.
>   Your price is based on credit sales—and I think
> it grossly unfair that a cash customer should foot
> the bill for the credit customer.
>   That's why we who pay cash no longer deal
> with you.
>   Don't you think that lowering your prices for
> cash might bring back your lost customers?
>   Sincerely yours,
>   *Your Name*
>   *Your Address*

Letters like this can also be used to combat other retail
outlets beside chain and department stores that won't honor
your UNCREDIT CARD.

It's the banks that are responsible for this cash discount resistance on the part of some of these outlets. Banks make money on their credit card sales, not on the retailers' cash sales. So while most retailers, as you've seen, are eager to give you discounts for cash, banks are even more eager to prevent the retailers from giving you those discounts. When, for example, about 100 retailers in California who had signed up with Master Charge, dropped their prices for payment with cash, "We were so darn mad," Mrs. Sandy Woodson, a Master Charge administrator admits, "[that] every one of them was either dropped . . . on a permanent basis, or so severely reprimanded that he never did it again."

To put legal teeth into their insistence that cash customers fare no better than credit card customers, many banks now include clauses in their credit card contracts with merchants that forbid cash discounts. But whether this restriction on trade comes contractually or by strong arm, it's hard to police, of questionable legality, and most retailers simply ignore it.

You will, however, find some retailers who will knuckle under to the banks, and stick to the letter of their contracts. And you'll find other merchants, who for their own reasons, will discard your UNCREDIT CARD. When you find these retailers, get your friends, relatives and neighbors to deluge them with letters telling them how they're losing business by not giving cash discounts in lieu of credit card sales. That hits them where it hurts.

Letters *do* work. Ask any politician or TV network executive. By using the kind of letter suggested here, and by getting other people to use it too, you *can* force the manager of your chain and department stores to give you discounts for cash, and you *can* force reluctant retailers to honor your UNCREDIT CARD. Fact is, there are few retail outlets where you can't, one way or another, get lower prices when you use your UNCREDIT CARD.

When you lower prices with your UNCREDIT CARD, you're acting not only for yourself, but for your entire community, and for all of us. Reason: You're helping fight *credit card inflation*. Not often discussed openly, credit card inflation is one of the root causes for our sky-rocketing prices. "Anyone engaged in consumer [price] protection is a hypocrite if he has a credit card," Ralph Nader told the National Commission on Consumer Finance. "I won't have a credit card," he added heatedly, "because it increases the cost of things to everyone."

An officer of a well known Manhattan clothing company agrees. "If we didn't have charges we'd go out of business because people demand them as convenience. But," he says, "there's no doubt that charges in general make everything cost more."

You've already seen how your retailer passed his credit card service fee, averaging 5 to 7 percent of the selling price, on to you. But that 5 to 7 percent is only part of the credit card bite. Your retailer also has to hand over an annual registration fee to the bank or T&E card company, and he has to pay for the use of the charge machine. In addition, as Nader's consumer credit specialist, Andy Spanogle, points out, credit cards always increase bookkeeping and administrative costs. And, strangely enough, very often your retailer has to go in hock to finance some of his credit card service. This happens when T&E card companies are very slow in paying him. When they hold up money for 30, 60, 90 days or more, your retailer becomes "cash poor." Since he can't operate without cash—"We prefer cash because we owe money to people and have to pay our bills," says the officer of the clothing company—your retailer has to go to the bank and borrow money. Borrowing money costs money. And that cost, like all the other credit card costs, is passed on to you.

Total up all those credit card costs. Add them to the price tag, and an item that cost you $100 *before* your retailer began to accept credit cards, costs you $110 immediately after he begins to accept credit cards. *The moment your retailer slaps a credit card decal on his window, his prices go up 10 percent!*

But that's only the start of the credit card price spiral. Retail prices are up, so wages must go up. But not just 10 percent. Wage increases must cover the higher taxes that come with higher income, and workers must be protected today for the price increases of tomorrow. A 10 percent boost in prices means boosts of 15, 20, 30 percent or more, in wages. And you know who pays for those wage increases? You do. The price of that $110 item leaps to $130.

Prices continue to *zoom*. Reason: Wage increases have boosted the prices of goods and services your retailer needs to operate his business. He has to write bigger checks for himself, too. Result: A price hike of another $10. That item which once sold for $100, then $110, then $130, now sells for $140. And the price still hasn't peaked out. Because—

With the latest boost, prices have again surged ahead of wages. Wages have to surge ahead of prices. But when wages rise, prices rise . . . when prices rise, wages rise . . . when wages rise, prices rise—and on and on with no end in sight. Project this inflationary spiral into the future, and a loaf of bread that cost 8¢ in 1948 could cost $8 or even $80 in 1978.

Of course, other causes contribute to the inflation that threatens the welfare and security of you and your family. There's the slump in individual productivity, the dollar-drain to the rackets, the gargantuan magnitude of government spending, the fiscal errors of the Federal Reserve, the cash squandered in featherbedding, the zooming budgets for advertising and election campaigns.

But while you, as an individual, can do very little to combat inflation stemming from these causes, *you* can *fight higher prices due to the credit card. And you can fight those prices —successfully. Others have already done it.*

So, like those others, take advantage of the credit card system to get lower prices for yourself, and help bring down prices for your community:

Waive your credit card.

Wave your UNCREDIT CARD.

It could be the banner of the price rebellion.

PART TWO

CON GAMES PLAYED WITH PLASTICS: THEY MAY BE INSIDE THE LAW

CHAPTER V

Credit Card Con Games (I)

How To Raise Big Dough To Play That Long Shot— And Never Have To Pay It Back

This is the story of how a young woman whose credit limit was $500 raised $5,000 with her credit cards. Then plunged it all on a gamble that could earn her $15,000 in one month—if she won; and if she lost—could cost her nothing. It's a caper that takes advantage of the loopholes in credit card service practices. But if you do need more money than you can borrow, and you're certain that you'll be able to pay it back, here, too, is a legitimate way you can raise thousands of dollars on your credit cards—even though your credit ceiling is low.

Janet X. Parker (a fictitious name) liked to go to the race track. Not to bet. But to watch the horses. She thought they were the most beautiful animals in the world. Seeing them up close was even more exciting to her than watching them race. She made up her mind to get into the stables. It wasn't easy. But she was determined and pretty, and she did it. She visited the stables every time she went to the track.

The jockeys liked her, and she got to know them well. She knew when one of them had a hangover, another had a spat with his wife, or when another was feeling high. Little things. Yet little things that could make a big difference. Like winning a horse race or losing it. Janet Parker knew the little things, and she knew when a jockey won and when he lost, and she began to put two and two together. She soon found she was able to pick some winners.

Could she do it consistently? she wondered. She made mental bets. She won and she lost. She lost and she won. But at the end of a couple of dozen bets she was ahead. She *could* do it consistently. Her next step: *real* bets.

Janet didn't have much money. She worked as a model. That's "iffy" work. Some days there are jobs. Most days there aren't. Janet didn't mind the leisure. It gave her time to go to the track. But she did mind the lack of money. Her hourly rate was high, but she worked so few hours that at the end of a year her earnings were less than a clerk's. All the money she had to bet was $50.

She bet it, the same way she had done mentally, over a couple of dozen races. She won. She reinvested in another couple of dozen races. She won again. She kept playing. At the end of about a hundred races, her $50 had grown to $150. It had taken her a month.

It seemed to Janet Parker that she had stumbled on a foolproof method for beating the ponies. It had come at the right time, too. She was going to be married soon. She had always had a dream about her wedding—it would be grand and glittering, and then afterwards, a luxuriously lazy honeymoon in the south of France. Up to now, she had thought it was a dream that could never come true. But here was her big chance to make it come true. She figured: If she could turn $50 into $150—*triple* her money—in a month, why couldn't she turn $5,000 into $15,000 in the same time? She *could,* she was certain, *if* she had the $5,000. But where was she to get that kind of money?

On the strength of her earnings, a signature loan for that amount from a bank or a finance company was out of the question. She had no friends or relatives flush enough to let her have the money, or even co-sign for the loan. She had nothing of value to pawn. The cash advances she could draw on her credit cards had already been drawn to help her keep going between jobs. She had no assets. But she did have one thing:

A stack of credit cards.

She couldn't get any more on them, but she could *buy things* with them. *And why not take the things I buy,* thought Janet Parker, *and turn them into cash by selling them. I don't have to pay for them until later, but in the meantime, I'll have the money, and I can use it to take my one big chance.*

"Is that *legal?*" her astonished fiance wanted to know when she told him about it. "Selling things you haven't even paid for?"

"Why shouldn't it be?" she answered.

She was honest. She had never failed to pay a debt when it was due in her life, and she had no intention of doing so now. But she knew she wouldn't have the money to pay for what she charged until—well, it would take about two weeks to sell what she bought, and she'd need another four weeks at the track—call it 45 days. If the bills came due before then, she couldn't pay them. So *Step One* in her plan was to see to it that the bills *didn't* come due before then.

She did this by riffling through her stack of cards and selecting the ones with the most distant billing dates (see Chapter II). If she bought on the 10th, she figured, with a bank card with a billing date *of* the 10th, she wouldn't be billed until the 10th *of the following month.* There were 30 days, plus the additional 25 days the banks gave her to pay the bill (before interest began to accrue at 18 percent per year, which she didn't want to pay), making 55 days in all. And since she'd *have* the money in 45 days, there was no question in her mind but that she'd win, she'd have no worry about paying off. And on time.

"But even if you can pay the money back on time," her fiance argued, "you still need $5,000 and they won't let you buy more than $500 on most of your credit cards. It won't work."

"Don't you worry about it," Janet Parket said confidently. "I've got it all worked out."

And she had.

Step Two in the Janet Parker Plan: As soon as she reached her limit on one credit card, she switched to another. She used about 20 cards. She found while she was using them that she could exceed most of their limits and get away with it. She did. In small amounts, $25 to $100, she went on a buying spree. In a few days, she had run up about $7,000 in charges. She only needed $5,000. But she had purposely overbought, because she knew that she would have to sell what she bought at a discount.

What she bought was vital to the success of her Plan, and that was *Step Three.* She was careful to buy only those items for which there was a ready market. At airline counters, she charged "open" airline tickets (that is, tickets without specific flights or passenger names indicated). At department and chain stores, and at speciality shops, she charged gift certificates. When gift certificates weren't available, she bought merchandise, then returned the merchandise for a merchandise credit slip (rather than a credit to her charge account).

In short, she bought "negotiable paper" which could be used by anybody, any time, to buy anything. The only hard goods she bought were items that she could handle with ease physically—like Accutrons, Leicas, KLH radios. She also went to coin stores and charged $10 gold pieces.

Step Four was the actual selling. She had no trouble. At discounts ranging from 10 to 30 percent, her line was irresistible to her friends, relatives, neighbors and business acquaintances. Within two weeks, she had converted her purchases to the $5,000 she needed, plus a bit more for expenses.

She was ready.

If she won, the $5,000 would bring her $15,000. She would take $7,000 of that to pay off her credit card bills on time, and that would leave her $8,000. With it, her life's dream—the lavish wedding, the fairy-tale honeymoon abroad —would come true.

"But if you lose," her fiance warned her, "you'll be saddled —*we'll* be saddled—with $7,000 worth of debts. Most of it we'll be paying 18 percent interest a year on. We'll never be able to do it. We'll be in debt for the rest of our lives."

"Don't worry about that either," said Janet Parker quietly. "We'll win, and I'll pay. But even if we lose, I'll try to pay it back somehow. And if we can't—well, we won't be hurt."

* * *

Janet Parker lost.

She lost every cent.

When the payments came due, she defaulted. She didn't want to, but she had to. The credit card collection departments closed in. Some went to court and got judgments against her. That meant they had a right now to seize her assets. But Janet Parker had no assets.

Except her salary. They tried to garnishee it. A garnishment is a legal order to an employer to deduct a certain amount of the employee's salary each pay day, and send it directly to the creditor until the debt is paid. But there's a new law: the Federal Wage Garnishment Restriction Law. It's designed to protect low income wage earners from crippling garnishments. When the employee's income is as low as Janet Parker's, the Law goes so far as to forbid any garnishment whatsoever. The bill collectors couldn't touch Janet Parker's salary.

But they could wait, since a judgment stays in effect for years. Her salary wasn't likely to go up, but there was always the chance she might acquire some property worth seizing, and when she did they'd pounce on her. But Janet Parker was going to be married. Therefore, if there was any property to be acquired, her husband would acquire it. And while it's true that a husband is responsible for his wife's debts, he's not responsible (except in community property states), if those debts were acquired before the marriage. Janet Parker did *not* live in a community property state, and her debts *were* acquired before her marriage. The bill collectors could wait forever, but they'd never be able to pounce on her.

Because Janet Parker had no assets, and because the law protected her against salary garnishment, she was judgment proof. And once she married, she *could stay* judgment proof for the rest of her life.

The banks and the credit card companies had dropped $7,000. But there was no way they could recover a penny of it.

Before she'd placed her bets, Janet Parker had worked all this out in her mind. She knew exactly what would happen in case she lost. "If I win," she'd told her fiance, "I win big. If I lose, I lose nothing."

*　　*　　*

Unfortunately for the credit card companies, Janet Parker found a plan that worked. *Was* that plan illegal? Become Janet Parker for the next few minutes. Look at the "plastics world" through her eyes, and see for yourself how she found the loopholes that made her plan possible, and why *she* believed that she had committed no crime.

If you're Janet Parker, to make your plan work, you need a large number of credit cards. The loophole is:

There is no limit imposed on the number of credit cards you can acquire.

And they're easy to get. Even on a low income.

You can get your first credit card with no fuss or feathers from your bank. Chances are, it sent you one in the mail, even though you never asked for it. When a bank introduces a credit card service, that's the way it gets its customers. Most bank credit cards in use today were sent out unsolicited. But if you don't get one in the mail, you can go to your bank and apply for one. Banks want your credit card business and they make it easy for you. An account in the bank to which you're applying is usually enough to get you an O.K. If you have no bank account, a history of steady employment, a permanent residence, and a telephone should do the trick. The telephone doesn't have to be entirely yours. You may be sharing an apartment and sharing the cost of the telephone, but if your name is listed in the phone book, you qualify.

You can get your second card at your local department store or discount house. Requirements are tougher than at your bank. But if you already have a bank card, that should get you the stamp of approval.

Now you have two credit cards—and they can be your open sesame to the nation's treasure house of credit cards. All you have to do is: Use them. But don't misuse them. Make sure you stay within your credit limits. If you can, pay before interest charges accumulate. If you can't, make sure you pay on your due dates. In short, keep your credit rating A-1 plus. Then when you apply for any other card, simply give either or both of your cards as references—and you're in.

There are hundreds of credit cards available in the U.S.A. They're yours for the asking. Most card holders carry at least six cards. The national average is about 20. Many Americans carry 40 cards or more.

If you're Janet Parker, to make your plan work, you have to exceed your credit card ceilings. The loophole is:

Credit card ceilings just can't be policed.

Congressional committees are concerned with the wild-fire spread of credit cards, particularly among segments of the population poorly equipped to meet the burden of regular payments at 12 to 18 percent interest per year. But the committees have been placated by credit card spokesmen who emphasize that most cards put a *low* dollar limit on what the card holder can charge. Andrew F. Brimmer, member of the Board of Governors of the Federal Reserve System, told the

Senate Subcommittee on Financial Institutions that, "The average line of credit extended under credit card plans is in the neighborhood of $350. This is not so high as to be a cause in itself of a customer's incurring excessive indebtedness."

Credit card spokesmen also point this out: Some ceilings on credit cards go as low as $100, almost none go higher than $500. Credit card users who elect to pay off at 10 percent of their unpaid balance monthly, are only obligated to meet payments of from $10 to $50 per month including interest. That's a modest debt burden that can be met by almost anyone qualified to hold a credit card.

But what the credit card spokesmen don't point out is that these ceilings are virtually meaningless. Credit card ceilings can't be policed. Card users exceed them frequently—either by accident or by intent. There's the *New York Post* story of a woman who charged over $1,600 on a bank card with a ceiling of $400. There are thousands of like stories.

Of course, if you overcharge consistently month after month, the credit card services are likely to crack down. But, certainly, anyone can get away with it big at least once, and modestly many times. Hint: Don't worry about exceeding the limit on the better known private company "expense account" cards: the sky's the limit.

If you're Janet Parker, to make your plan work, you need to use about 20 cards at the same time. The loophole is:

There is no limit to the number of credit cards you can use at the same time.

That's something else the credit card spokesmen don't point out when they reassure the legislators with statistics on low ceilings. A ceiling may be low, but multiplied many times, it goes out of sight. Use 30 cards, each with a limit of only $100, and you're in hock for $3,000. Use 30 cards, each with a ceiling of $400, and you've charged up $12,000. But jack up that ceiling, as the woman in the *New York Post* story did, to $1,600, and you can go on a buying spree to the tune of $48,000. And you may not have a cent to your name when you do it.

Splurge with several of the no-limit expense account cards simultaneously, and the totals you can run up boggle the imagination. As it is, unpaid monthly balances on these cards hover around the $2,500 mark. For *each* card. And every American who holds this kind of card usually holds more than one.

Now you come to the heart of the Janet Parker plan. If you're Janet Parker, to make your plan work, you need the right to *sell* your credit card purchases, even though you haven't made a single payment on them. The loophole is:

The moment the sales clerk accepts your credit card, legal title to the merchandise passes to you.

The merchandise you buy with your credit card is yours. You can do anything you please with it. You can keep it, or give it away, or burn it. Or *sell* it.

This is not true of other types of credit purchases. So be careful. Buy a car from a dealer on the basis of a down payment plus monthly payments, sell the car before you've made your last payment, and you can go to jail. Your house is not all yours until you've paid off the mortgage. You can't sell it, unless you deduct the amount you owe on the mortgage from the sales price. Don't try, either, to dispose of furniture, appliances or the color TV you've bought on a time-purchase plan at your local store. Nothing you buy that way belongs to you until every payment is paid in full. The same is true when you acquire a typewriter on a lease-purchase agreement. It's often illegal even to take the typewriter out of your premises; and you can end up in the magistrate's court if you do.

What's more, on many of these *credit* purchases—but not credit *card* purchases—the seller can repossess the merchandise at any time for non-payment. Remember: On most *credit* purchases, the property probably belongs to the store, not to you, until you pay in full. Pay all the payments except the last, default on that one, and the hi-fi you've sweated to keep up payments on for a year and a half, gets whisked out of your possession. On credit *card* purchases, however, the merchandise *is* yours, and your retailer can *not* repossess, even if you don't make a single payment.

So plunk down your plastic. What you charge, you own then and there, and it can never be taken away from you if you don't come across with the cash. It's a situation without precedent or parallel in the credit world, and it can only exist because of the credit card. Here's why:

When you charge with a credit card, your retailer is paid by the credit card service. In reality, this means the credit card service advances *you* the money to make the purchase. So you *do* pay with your credit card, even though you don't do the paying. And what you pay for belongs to you. Moreover, the money is advanced to you without any strings attached on what you buy. The credit card service has no claims on your purchases. If you default on payments, the credit card service can sue you for the money it advanced, but it can *not* repossess the merchandise you bought with the money.

This is why it's quite safe—and within your rights—to *charge* and cash in your charges before any cash goes out.

If you're Janet Parker, to make your plan work, you should be sure you won't be burdened with catastrophic debt in case you lose. The loophole is:

If you can't pay the credit card services, they can't collect.

Or, simply stated: they can't get blood out of a stone. Since your credit card creditors can't repossess the merchandise you bought, their only recourse is to obtain judgments against you, try to garnishee your wages, seize your assets. But new state and federal laws severely restrict the amounts of money that can be deducted from your salary. And more and more Americans are "taking" the credit card services by protecting their assets through marriage (see Chapter VII). There's a rising tide of judgment proof credit card holders. What's the reaction of the credit card services to them? They try their hardest to collect, but, one top credit card executive concedes, "If they can't pay . . . or won't pay . . . we just forget it."

*   *   *

You've just seen the loopholes as Janet Parker saw them. Remember, you're not Janet Parker, but by seeing the "plastics world" the same way she did, you can see why Janet Parker believed she had violated no law. And it's true that while each of her actions was shady, none was outside the law. But put them all together and wasn't there a clear intent to defraud the credit card companies in case she lost? That's a crime. But, "I never intended to defraud anybody," Janet Parker would argue. "I intended to pay. I just couldn't. Debt isn't a crime." So there you are—a con game that may be legal. Or may not be. Says the chief of the Fraudulent Claims Bureau of the Massachusetts Division of Insurance, "We know how to deal with the criminal element, but the suburbanite with larceny in his heart offers a more difficult problem." And the credit card is making that problem even more difficult.

The Janet Parker story is not one girl's story, but a composite of dozens of true-life experiences of ordinary people who have taken advantage of loopholes in the credit card system to take their one big chance (or their one big fling: Travel around the world, live in luxury, fling gifts around like a Rajah)—without taking a cent out of their own pockets. They used the money of the credit card services. But in the long run, it isn't the credit card services who pay when the "Janet Parker's" don't pay—it's *you*. Here's why:

Losses on credit cards due to non-payment are 20 times higher than on personal bank loans—and con games help keep them that high. What the credit card services do to compensate for these mountainous losses is to smack your retailer with staggering fees. (This is why they can afford to "just forget it" when a con man or a deadbeat refuses to pay.) *And those fees are passed on to you—whether you pay with credit cards or with cash* (see Chapter IV).

You know who the real victim of every credit card con game is?

You.

*   *   *

But if you need more money than you can borrow or raise by a cash advance with your bank card, there is a legitimate way to get it.

Background:

Chances are you have a BankAmericard or a Master Charge card or both. Did you know that you can get *two* BankAmericards? Or *three?* Or *six?* Or *more? Not* copies. Distinct, separate cards. All made out to you, all carrying your name, but each bearing a *different* account number. And the same goes for Master Charge. It's a little known fact, but it's a fact. You can get a BankAmericard from *any* bank issuing BankAmericards. You can get a Master Charge card from *any* bank issuing Master Charge cards.

Action:

Step One. Obtain as many bank cards as you can. If you're in New York, for example, go to the Manufacturer's Hanover Trust and get a Master Charge. Then go to the First National City Bank and get another. Then go to the Chemical Bank and add a third. And so on. Make a collection of Bank-Americards the same way.

Step Two. Now—*charge!* But not merchandise. Cash. You can't get more than a $500 advance on any card, but *use enough cards* and you can raise, say, $5,000.

Drawback, though:

To get several thousand dollars, you need many cards, and there may not be that many banks in the neighborhoods in which you live and work from which to get them (outside those neighborhoods, you'll have trouble getting any cards at all). For example, the maximum cash advance allowed by a major bank card system is $500. To raise $5,000 on its cards means you'll need 10 cards, 10 banks. And if you use bank cards with lower credit ceilings, you'll need even more banks. Remember: we're talking about banks, *not* branches. You can get only one card per bank, no matter how many branches it has. Each bank must be a separate institution. And how many banks *are* there in the vicinity of your home and place of business? Fact is, the "Multiple Bank Card Plan" for raising cash is only likely to work in or around big cities.

Advice:

If you use the Multiple Bank Card Plan, be sure you can pay the money back. Remember, you not only have to pay back the capital—but you'll also have to pay it back with interest at 12 percent per year. And if you don't draw your advances with prudence, you may find that you'll be overspending. If you're not careful, you may end up by playing a credit card con game—on yourself.

CHAPTER VI

Credit Card Con Games (II)

How to Get Cash at No Cost— And Earn up to 155 Percent Per Year on It

If you're a retailer, what do you do when you request a loan, and the banks say "no"? You raise the cash from the banks—with your friends' and relatives' credit cards. And you don't pay a cent of interest. That's a new credit card con game that gets "loans" from banks even though the banks don't know they're making the "loans." Then the retailer takes the interest free money and puts it to work to earn more money at a fabulous rate of interest. But without resort to this questionable practice, you can get similar results. To follow the details, you've got to face up to a little arithmetic —but when the figures show up in black on your bottom line, chances are you'll decide it was worth it.

Imagine that you're Fred Adams.

You're a small retailer, Mr. Adams.

With a big problem.

It's a dollar and cents problem, and this is it—you have monthly bills to pay amounting to $4,000. In your industry, you can pay in full on the 30th, or take an 8 percent discount on the 10th. Eight percent of $4,000 is $320. Over a year, that's $320 x 12 or $3,840—and that's a sizeable saving. But you can't save it, because the way cash flows into your business, you never have sufficient funds on the 10th to take the discount. So it's a $3,840-a-year problem—and what are you going to do about it?

As recently as two years ago, you could do something about it easily. You could go to a bank and get the money to pay your bills by the 10th and take the discount. You knew that by the end of the month, your business would bring in sufficient funds to pay the bank back. All you needed was $3,680 ($4,000 less $320) from the 10th to the 30th—and the bank was glad to give it to you. You paid for it, of course. At about 10 percent per year. But for 20 days, that amounted to only about $21; and to pay $21 to save $320, left you with no kick coming. It was a good deal.

But that was two years ago. Today, the "credit crunch" has caught up with you. The bank finds it far more profitable to finance consumer credit card sales than to make small business loans. "Sorry," your Loan Officer will tell you, "we just don't have enough money to go around." So you've got to raise that $3,680 by the 10th of the month another way.

Here's that way in its simplest form:

Step One. Pick three friends and relatives on whom you can rely. Make sure each of them holds three bank cards. Make sure that your store honors the bank cards that they hold.

Step Two. On the 9th, have them come into your store and *charge!* about $435 worth of merchandise on each of their cards. Make sure all the charge slips are deposited before 3 p.m. on the 10th. Now follow the arithmetic: Three people with three cards each, that's nine cards. Nine times $435 is a bit more than $3,900. The bank takes 5 percent of that. That leaves you with $3,680 (and a few bucks extra). That's the money you need. The bank credits that money to your bank account on the 10th. You're in. You use the money to take your discounts.

Step Three. Between the 10th and the 30th, as cash flows in because of sales, make deposits in your account of $3,680.

Step Four. On the 29th, see to it that the merchandise your friends and relatives bought on the 9th is *returned* for full credit to their bank credit card accounts. Charging the merchandise, therefore, cost them nothing. When you deposit the credit slips on the 30th, the bank deducts the $3,680 from your account. But you've already deposited $3,680 in cash to cover the deduction, so there's no problem. The bank gets its money back. But *from the 10th to the 30th you have had the use of the bank's money. You have had it without interest or any other cost. In essence, you have been given a 20-day "loan"—free of charge.*

*   *   *

You've used the "Charge-and-Return" plan to meet a cash emergency in your business, Mr. Adams. Now you're going to use that plan *at the same time* to build capital funds to eliminate that emergency. And if you were writing a how-to-do-it manual on the method, it would go something like this:

Background: You return to the situation where you have $4,000 in bills discountable on the 10th at 8 percent. You know you'll be able to pay those bills *in full* on the 30th. That means, you'll have $4,000 on the 30th, not just $3,680. That $4,000 is the key, remember it.

Action:

Step One. Have your friends and relatives charge up $4,000 in merchandise by the 10th. The bank takes its bite of 5 percent ($200) and credits your account with $3,800 ($4,000 minus $200).

Step Two. On the tenth, take advantage of the 8 percent discount ($320), and pay your bills. Remember that costs you $3,680 ($4,000 minus $320).

Step Three. By the 30th, deposit credit slips for the merchandise your friends and relatives return. The bank now deducts the $3,800 it had credited you with 20 days before.

Step Four. In those 20 days, you had deposited not just $3,800, but *$4,000*. If you hadn't used the Charge-and-Return Plan, you'd be paying out that $4,000 on the 30th. The entire $4,000 would be wiped out. But by using the plan, you were able to pay your bills on the 10th with only $3,680. The plan, therefore, has given you a profit of $320 ($4,000 minus $3,680)! That's a profit of 8 percent on $4,000. And you made that profit on the *bank's* money, for which you paid nothing!

Step Five. Your $320 profit is in your bank account. Keep it there.

Step Six. The next month, you're once again faced with $4,000 worth of bills which you can clear up on the 10th for $3,680. But this month, you already have $320 in the bank, so all you need is $3,360 ($3,680 minus $320). Therefore, your friends and relatives don't have to charge up as much as the month before. Get them to charge up $3,600 (instead of $4,000). That'll net you (since you must deduct 5 percent of $3,600 which is $180) $3,420. This is a bit more than the $3,360 you need. Pay off the $3,680 on the 10th, pay back your bank "loan" with credit slips for returned merchandise by the 30th, deposit $4,000 in cash by the 30th. Once again, you've made a profit of $320 ($4,000 minus $3,680)! Keep it in your bank account.

Step Seven. The next month, you repeat the procedure. But this time, you start with two months' profits $640 ($320 plus $320). Your friends and relatives only have to charge $3,200 worth of merchandise. Five percent of that is $160, so you'll net $3,040 ($3,200 minus $160). Add $640 to that and you get $3,840, again more than the $3,680 you need to meet your bills on the 10th. You meet them, and at the end of the month, you've added another $320 in profits to your bank account.

Step Eight. Repeat the procedure every month for a year, following this chart:

HOW TO INCREASE YOUR CAPITAL
AT NO COST TO YOU

Month	Your friends and relatives charge	You net by the 10th (charge less 5%)	Your monthly profit is (8% of $4,000)	Your profit added from month to month totals	The amount of cash you have by the 10th is* (you need $3,680)
1st	$4,000	$3,800	$320	$ 320	$3,800
2nd	$3,600	$3,420	$320	$ 640	$3,740
3rd	$3,200	$3,040	$320	$ 960	$3,680
4th	$2,900	$2,755	$320	$1,280	$3,715
5th	$2,600	$2,470	$320	$1,600	$3,750
6th	$2,200	$2,090	$320	$1,920	$3,690
7th	$1,900	$1,805	$320	$2,240	$3,725
8th	$1,600	$1,520	$320	$2,560	$3,760
9th	$1,200	$1,140	$320	$2,880	$3,700
10th	$ 900	$ 855	$320	$3,200	$3,735
11th	$ 600	$ 570	$320	$3,520	$3,770
12th	$ 200	$ 190	$320	$3,840	$3,710

To arrive at this figure add the "net" (third column from the left) to the preceding month's "total profit" (fifth column from the left.)

You'll note that your cash needs (third column from the left in the chart) become less pressing month after month. At the end of 12 months, you'll have increased your capital by $3,840—more than enough to pay off your bills on the 10th without any help at all. This means that the money you've earned will continue to earn you 8 percent on $4,000 every month thereafter.

You've earned this money at an astonishing yearly rate. Just a bit more arithmetic to prove it. That 8 percent discount: on a $100 invoice, that's $8. Now, if you have an invoice that can be satisfied by $92 on the 10th of the month, but you satisfy it with $100 on the 30th, you're really paying $8 to borrow $92 for 20 days. To find the true interest, according to the Truth in Lending Law, divide 8 by 92. That gives you 8.7 percent—and that's your true interest rate for 20 days. Thirty days is one and one-half times longer, so the monthly rate is (8.7 x 1½) a little over 13 percent. Multiply 13 by 12 and you get your yearly earning rate, and that's—*155 percent!* That's sensational in itself, but it's even more sensational when you consider that the money you earn it on comes to you free of charge.

* * *

But this entire "Fred Adams caper" hinges on the trick of getting friends and relatives to charge-and-return. Is this legal? To Fred Adams (it's a fictitious name, but the story is based on fact) the answer is, "Why isn't it?" He points out that if you're a retailer:

Whenever any customer charges on a bank card, then returns what she's charged, you have the use of the bank's money during the period she's kept the merchandise. Example: Your customer buys $500 worth of merchandise on the 15th, returns it for full credit on the 20th. You've had the use of $475 ($500 less 5 percent) for five days without interest costs. These charge-and-returns happen to every retailer as a matter of course, so he's constantly being granted "free" loans. When you use the Charge-and-Return Plan you're simply taking advantage of this loophole in the credit card system.

But is the argument valid? When he connives with his friends and relatives to charge-and-return, isn't Fred Adams getting money under false pretenses? When he uses the bank's money at no cost, isn't he depriving the bank of income it could have earned on that money? Again, as in the case of Janet X. Parker, it's a tricky legal question. Fred Adams may be within the law. He may not. But if you're a retailer, and you're in a cash squeeze like Fred Adams, you don't have to risk this questionable procedure. To get out of a cash squeeze you can do it above board—*with* credit cards. There are two ways.

One way:

You can use the Mulitple Bank Card Plan described in the preceding chapter. Raise the $3,680 you need by cash advances.

The Multiple Bank Card Plan differs in this respect from the Charge-and-Return Plan; it costs money. On bank card cash advances, the banks charge you 12 percent per year. Are the dollars you get worth the price you pay for them? If you're using the dollars to build capital by taking advantage of the 10th-of-the-month discounts, the answer is a resounding *yes*. Of course, your rate of earnings depends on your 10th-of-the-month discount rate. In the ladies garment industry, 8 percent is normal. In some other industries the rates are lower, and in others, higher. But whatever the rates, you can put them to work for you in conjunction with the Charge-and-Return Plan to increase your capital at no cost to you.

Use the money you raise with the Multiple Bank Card Plan to take your 8 percent profit on $4,000 each month, and here's the profit-versus-cost recap:

HOW TO INCREASE YOUR CAPITAL
WITH BANK CREDIT CARD ADVANCES

Month	You get advances of	Your monthly gross profit is (8% of $4,000)	Your advances cost you (12% per year for 20 days)	Your monthly net profit is (gross profit less cost of advances)	Your profit added from month to month totals
1st	$3,680	$320	$24.19	$295.81	$ 295.81
2nd	$3,384	$320	$22.90	$297.10	$ 592.91
3rd	$3,088	$320	$20.30	$299.70	$ 892.61
4th	$2,787	$320	$18.32	$301.68	$1,194.29
5th	$2,485	$320	$16.34	$303.66	$1,497.95
6th	$2,182	$320	$14.34	$305.66	$1,803.61
7th	$1,876	$320	$12.33	$307.67	$2,111.28
8th	$1,568	$320	$10.31	$309.69	$2,420.97
9th	$1,260	$320	$ 8.28	$311.72	$2,732.69
10th	$ 958	$320	$ 6.30	$313.70	$3,046.39
11th	$ 634	$320	$ 4.17	$315.83	$3,362.22
12th	$ 318	$320	$ 2.09	$317.91	$3,680.13
			Total Cost $159.87		*Total Profit* $3,680.13

So for a total cost of $159.87, you make $3,680.13. Not bad. But the cost isn't even as high as that. The chart assumes that you deposited the $4,000 on the 30th. This is to say, you paid back your advances (and took your profit) in 20 days, so the interest is calculated for 20 days. Actually, though, receipts are coming in daily, so you can pay off your advances *as the receipts come in*. This shortens the average time of the loan to about 10 days—and that cuts the interest cost in half. You only need to spend $79.94 to make $3,680.13. Not bad? Darn good!

A final thought about the Multiple Bank Card Plan—

As an established businessman, you could have solved your money problem by obtaining a *personal* bank loan for $3,680. You wouldn't even have minded paying the sky high 18 percent a year interest, since you would earn at the rate of 155 percent a year with the money it bought. But borrowing with multiple bank cards has the advantages of no forms to fill out, no credit investigation, no questions asked, no delays.

A second way for you, as a retailer, to escape the credit crunch and keep the cash flowing in without resorting to a credit card con game is to use the *Reverse* UNCREDIT CARD Plan.

Remember, the UNCREDIT CARD Plan (see Chapter IV) is based on two hard core facts of the credit card system: (1) that banks take 5 percent of sales on their credit cards, and T&E card services take 7 percent; and (2) that your customer pays the same price for an item whether he uses a credit card or pays cash.

Your customer presents the deal by handing over his credit card and his UNCREDIT CARD at the same time. The message on the UNCREDIT CARD tells you that your customer is willing to waive his credit card and pay cash in return for a discount. When he pays in cash, you don't have to pay the 5 to 7 percent credit card fee, so you're willing to split that fee with him. You cut your expense and, consequently, up your profit.

That's the UNCREDIT CARD Plan. In the *Reverse* UN-

CREDIT CARD Plan, *you* tell the customer that if he'll waive his *T&E* cards and pay for cash, *you'll give him* a discount. T&E cards only. Because what you're after is ready cash, and a charge on a bank card is like ready cash; deposit today's charge slips before 3 P.M. and your account is credited with them today. But T&E credit card companies make you wait and wait and wait for your money. If you can convert a T&E card sale into cash, you're ahead of the game.

The same fee-splitting holds as in the UNCREDIT CARD Plan, and you gain in the same way. You can offer discounts ranging from 3½ to 6 percent and still come up with at least an extra 1 percent in your pocket. But if your customer needs stronger persuasion to waive his T&E card, offer discounts up to the full amount you would have had to pay the T&E credit card services: 7 percent. You'll lose nothing and you'll gain the cash.

Here's how to make the *Reverse* UNCREDIT CARD Plan presentation. When your T&E card customer says, "Charge it," you say something like: "If you come back in five days with the cash, I'll give you a discount of 3½ percent. In the meantime, the merchandise is yours. I won't put the charge in for five days, so, if you don't come in with the cash, you get five *extra* days free credit. If you do come in with the cash, you get the merchandise at a reduced price. How can you lose?"

Chances are your dollar-wise customer will take advantage of those five extra free credit days, and come in on the fifth day with the cash. When she does, why don't you take even further advantage of the situation with a little speech like this?

"Madam, it's good to see someone who still pays with cash. Since I have to give the credit card company a kickback on every credit card sale, I'm going to give you the kickback instead. I promised you a 3½ percent discount. I'm going to give you what I would have had to give the credit card company. That's 7 percent."

You give away nothing that you wouldn't have given away to the T&E card company had she used her card. You *get* the cash. And you'll have made a friend. And a repeat customer, who'll waive her T&E card again and again to help keep *you* supplied with cash. With enough customers like her, you should be able to raise all the cash you need to profit from your 10th-of-the-month discounts.

An added benefit: By encouraging your customers to pay cash, you could help break the 5 to 7 percent stranglehold the credit card services have on you.

CHAPTER VII

Credit Card Con Games (III)

How to Wipe Out Credit Card Debts Without Paying Them— And Start Life Anew With $30,000 Free and Clear

Here's a stunt used by hopelessly in debt card holders to charge up thousands of dollars more, then take the money and run. Here, too, is how thousands of Americans plan to avoid paying unmanageable credit card debts before they get into debt. How others get rid of their debts at a discount, and how still others sidestep salary garnishments. But you can fight unmanageable credit card debt without reliance on these shady operations. Use the aides you'll find in this chapter: a simple test to discover whether you're "debt-prone," and a formula to calculate how much you can charge each month without getting into trouble. Plus: an infallible method to beat unmanageable credit card debt forever—and save money besides.

Joe Loomis is an electronics engineer. Up to six months ago, he was employed in an $18,000-a-year job on the circuitry of a spacecraft computer. That's the only job he ever had. That's all he knows: how to design parallax correction parameters for hyperbolic orbital functions. With the cutback in the space program, there's not another job like it in the country. Joe Loomis is also 42 years old. At the employment agencies, they tell him it's a waste of time to fill out an application.

He has a wife and two kids, and he's willing to work at anything. But his firm is located in an industrial park 80 miles from the nearest big city, and the recession that's closed down Joe Loomis' plant has closed down most of the others, too. It's a ghost town. Joe Loomis lives in a small house a few miles from the plant. There's no work for him at all in the neighborhood. He can't commute to the big city; it's too far away. Joe Loomis is unemployable.

He's also in debt. Most of it credit card debt. While he was working, he never thought for a moment that the nation would ever slash funds for space exploration. If ever there was an industry of the future, space exploration was it, and Joe Loomis banked his future on it. His rented house was a showcase of the kind of good living the credit card can buy. Yet, he hadn't overspent. If his job hadn't been pulled out from under him, he could easily have made the extended payments as they came due. But now the credit card services were threatening, "Unless you pay by return mail, we will be forced to turn this matter over to our attorneys for collection."

If they did, Joe Loomis knew, all past installments must be paid immediately. That was according to the conditions of his credit card contract as set forth in the "disclosure sheet" which the credit card services were required by law to send him. But Joe Loomis also knew, from the experiences of his neighbors and former co-workers, that when the lawyers sued, they didn't sue only for the back payments, but for the total balance which amounted to $4,000. And that wasn't all he'd have to pay. "If any amount due and payable is referred for collection to an attorney, you will be required to pay court costs and an attorney's fee . . . *equal to 20 percent of the indebtedness,"* his BankAmericard disclosure sheet warned him; and his other credit card disclosure sheets were just as menacing. Because he couldn't pay $4,000 through no fault of his own, he would have to pay $4,800.

He couldn't raise that kind of money. If attorneys sued, they'd get a judgment against him. Whatever remained of his savings would be wiped out, his house would be stripped bare and almost everything in it put up for sale. *Everything* —because, he also knew from people who had gone through it, in a forced sale like this he would be lucky if his household goods went for 10 percent of what he'd paid for them. He was in a spot. Here's how he got out of it:

First, he wrote to the credit managers of the credit card services, enclosing one back payment to each (virtually washing out his remaining savings); telling them that he intended to resume regular payments and he'd catch up with back payments as soon as possible. That bought him time. The threatening letters wouldn't arrive again for another month or more. Then, he drove into the big city and visited the Australian consulate.

Teachers, particularly of technical subjects, are in great demand in Australia, and for the past two months Joe Loomis was dickering for a job teaching electronics in a high school in the suburbs of Sydney. The school had accepted him, but he hadn't been sure he wanted to uproot his family. Now, he told the Australian consul, he *was* sure, and he'd like to leave as quickly as possible. The consul arranged for a flight leaving for Sydney in three weeks. The fare for the entire Loomis family would be paid by the Australian government.

That would get them as far as Sydney, but all the cash Loomis had left was less than $100. He needed a nest egg to start a new life in a strange country. In his circumstances, he realized, the only way he could get that nest egg was to use his credit cards. He had used up all the cash advances on the cards he had, so he decided to use the Multiple Bank Card Plan (see Chapter VIII). He'd get as many *different* BankAmericards and Master Charge cards as he could by applying for them at *different* banks. These were not duplicates of his own cards, but cards with *different* account numbers. There were many banks in the big city, and he found that even though he lived 80 miles away, it didn't stop him from getting the cards. The banks regarded the big city as the nearest shopping center to the industrial park, and the park was, therefore, an economic part of the city. He got around the *"Employed by: ...."* line on the application form by not writing "unemployed," but rather "self-employed." This was true, since he had been called in, on several occasions, as a consultant by a near-by electronics firm. And on the line *"Earnings: ...."* he filled in, quite honestly, the sum he expected to earn from the Australian government. Joe Loomis also found that although his accounts were in arrears, he still wasn't blackballed, and that the delinquent cards he held actually got him quick O.K.'s on the cards he wanted. He was able to get three new BankAmericards, four Master Charge cards, and one Uni-Card. He charged up maximum cash advances on each of them. He was ahead by nearly $4,000.

Then, with all his cards, his new ones as well as his old ones, he pulled the Janet Parker caper (see Chapter V). He bought "negotiable paper"—airline tickets, merchandise credit slips, gift certificates—and easily saleable merchandise. He charged appreciably over the $400 to $500 ceilings on his credit limit cards, and ran up thousands of dollars on his T&E cards. The things he bought were his to sell, and he sold them. No trouble finding buyers at the discounts he offered. On the same terms, he sold everything in his home he had bought previously with his credit cards, except clothes. He also sold his car and all other property that he could find a market for. By the time the plane took off for Sydney, he had $30,000 in Barclay's traveler's checks in his pocket.

When he got to Australia, Joe Loomis intended to pay back the credit card services from his salary and the return on the investments he'd make with his nest egg. But he knew that if the situation ever arose again when he couldn't pay, none of the credit card services that he owed money to would be able to collect from him in Australia. Debt is not a criminal act, therefore nobody can be extradited; that is, forceably returned from a foreign country to face trial. As long as Joe Loomis remained in Australia, he would be, for all practical purposes, safe from credit card collectors—even if he were never able to pay back a cent.

*   *   *

The "skip thief"—the deadbeat who runs up bills then "skips" to the next town, changes his name and then starts all over again—has long been a familiar figure to law enforcement officers all over the nation. Since the first private detective agency went into business just after the Civil War, "skip tracing" has been one of the major pursuits of the private eye. Yet, despite continual official and unofficial police surveillance, the skip thief is better off now than he's ever been. The credit card has provided him not only with an easy means of cleaning out the town, but also of getting out of town. Or out of the country. And no one would know for months that he'd taken the money and run. Except for the fact that the Australian government, and not the credit card services, paid for his passage abroad, Joe Loomis acted precisely like a skip thief. As a matter of fact, had Joe Loomis *planned* to defraud the credit card services he would *be* a skip thief, and he could be sent back to America for trial and a stiff jail sentence.

But Joe Loomis (it's a fictitious name, and his story is constructed from many stories) is not a crook. He's just one of the many Americans who find the pressures of life in this country too much to cope with and use the credit card system as an escape valve. Usually, they have no criminal intent. The draft dodger who runs up charges of several thousand dollars in cash before fleeing to Canada is determined to pay every last cent off—once he gets a job. The magazine editor who's fed up with America and goes off to Rome to write, never dreams that he won't be able to pay back the grub stake of cash, clothes, transportation and a portable typewriter—once he begins to sell his work The poor young couple who think it's fun to live so cheaply in Spain on American money raised with their credit cards, never doubt they'll meet installments—once their little boutique begins to show a profit. But they're all gambling, just as surely as if they were panning for gold, and when things don't pan out, it's the credit card services that'll be hurt—just as badly as if they had been worked over by a team of professional skip thieves.

A *New York Times* survey tells us that more and more Americans, finding life intolerable here, are going abroad to live. It's likely that many of them will find the credit card a painless—and, perhaps, a payless—way to start a new life.

*   *   *

So, the American who makes his home abroad and can't pay the credit card debts he contracted for back in the States, is home free. Provided he hadn't set out with intent to defraud. Even though the final results to the credit card services are the same as if he had.

Back home, many Americans have found other ways to escape credit card debts when they can't pay them. All these ways are within the law. Here's one:

Long before the card holder charges up a single item, he transfers all his tangible assets—his savings, his insurance, his stocks, his car, his house, his household furniture—to his wife. Then when he defaults on his debts, and the credit card services get a judgment against him and attempt to seize his assets, they find he has no assets to seize. He's made himself *judgment-proof.* He's prepared *in advance* to avoid payment in case he couldn't come up with the cash.

The law says that's legitimate, provided he doesn't make the transfer with the intent to evade payment of debt. And how does the law know when he doesn't? By fixing the time of the transfer. If the transfer is made *before* debts are incurred, obviously there can be no intent at evasion, because how can he evade debts when there are no debts to evade? The rule of law was constructed before the credit card made future debts as real as present ones.

Danger: The card holder makes himself judgment-proof to prevent a financial cataclysm in case he runs up bills that become unmanageable due to circumstances beyond his control—a falling stock market, for example. But knowing that immunity from payment is assured, the judgment-proof card holder is tempted to run up bills that become unmanageable even when stocks are rising—particularly when the temptation comes in the form of plastic lures that entice him to buy, and buy, and buy only the best. *Uni-Card/ it isn't hard/you don't have to settle for second best/Uni-Card,* is the siren song of one commercial. Many Americans just don't have the will power it takes to resist this provocation to runaway overspending when they know that judgment-proofing will save them from financial disaster in case they can't meet their obligations. It's like "an invitation to crime without punishment," one judgment-proof card holder told us. "Do you wonder our resistance breaks down?" And when their resistance breaks down, and they can't come up with payments, it's the credit card services that take the punishment.

If the wife tries the scheme, though, it won't work. She can transfer all her property to her husband, but when she gets hit with a judgment, there's no protection. Her husband is responsible for her debts, and the credit card services not only seize the property she's transferred but her husband's property as well.

The loophole in this legislation, which appears to discriminate against women, is this: If the wife incurred her debts *before* her marriage, her husband is not responsible for them. Credit card companies suffer severe losses from young women who charge up large bills, transfer the goods they've charged to the men they're going to marry, then get married and quit their jobs. They plan to pay; but when the family budget dreamed up before the wedding bells, breaks up under the strain of the post-wedding bills, they just can't pay, and the credit card services just can't do a thing about it. *These* wives are judgment-proof.

*   *   *

It's difficult for anybody, though, to be truly judgment-proof if he/she is earning money. Earnings are assets that can be easily seized. A man who owns his own business may be able to beat the rap. Everything's in his wife's name to begin with, and so far as salary goes, his wife draws the salary, not he. But the ordinary wage earner can't transfer his salary to his wife. His wife has no way to protect her salary either. And both salaries can be *garnisheed*—which means, the employer is required by law to take a cut out of the debtor's salary and send it directly to the creditor. Yet, under certain circumstances, garnishment can be avoided, and the debtor can go on working and taking home a full paycheck, leaving the credit card services holding the bag.

Basis for this freedom from garnishment is the new Federal Wage Garnishment Restriction Law, which became effective July 1, 1970. It determines just how much money can be cut out of the debtor's salary. Follow these figures:

The debtor earns $150 a week. After taxes are deducted, he takes home $120 (the government calls this "disposable income"). There are two ways of calculating the amount of that $120 which the credit card service can garnishee. First way: Take 25 percent of $120. That's $30. Second way: Take the $120 and subtract from it $48. That's $72. The garnishment is for the lesser amount—$30, not $72.

Actually, the second way was written into the law to protect the *very* low income employee. The first $48 of disposable income is not subject to garnishment. Example: The debtor's salary is $70 a week. After taxes, it's $60. Use the two ways to calculate the amount of the garnishee. First way: Take 25 percent of $60. That' $15. Second way: Take $60 and subtract $48. That's $12. The garnishment is for the lesser amount—$12, not $15.

Note that when the salary was higher, the first way gave the lesser amount; when the salary was lower, the second way. As the salary gets lower and lower, the second way cuts the amount of garnishment down further and further: at $55 disposable income, the garnishment is $7 ($55 minus $48); at $50 disposable income, it's $2; ($50 minus $48); and when the disposable income dips to $48, the amount of garnishment becomes $0.00 ($48 minus $48). For any disposable income below $48, the amount of garnishment is also nothing.

If the debtor takes home, after taxes, no more than $48 a week, he's *garnishment-proof.* If a debtor takes home, after taxes, no more than $48 a week, and he has no other assets, he's *garnishment-proof* and *judgment-proof.* And there are hundreds of thousands of Americans in this financial category *who hold credit cards.* Most of the plastics are bank cards which came to them unsolicited in the mail. This proliferation of credit cards in the hands of people who are not legally responsible for their debts is a major source of concern to the credit card executives whose job it is to collect on delinquent accounts. The very fact that a Federal Law was necessary to pull the working poor out of debt, these experts stress, shows how widespread overspending among them had become. They foresee no diminution of that overspending in the future. On the contrary, they view the newly acquired freedom from garnishment as a spur to spending *more* than before. Credit cards in the hands of men and women taking home $48 a week and less, they point out, can provoke wild charging binges, particularly since the card holders know that when they can't afford to pay any of it back, they don't have to.

Danger of abuses arising from the new Federal Wage Garnishment Restriction Law also comes from students, and from young men and women who live in groups of four to six to keep expenses down while they're getting started in the arts or professions—all of whom support themselves with temporary work ("temporary personnel" is a billion dollar industry in the U.S.A.). Their disposable incomes seldom top $50-$60 a week. These young adults, often with sophisticated tastes, charge up thousands of dollars in luxury goods, travel and entertainment on the bright expectations of their futures. Too often, those futures are far from bright—and the credit card services get stuck. "These kids know the score, and the threat of garnishment used to keep their spending in line," one credit manager told us. "But I hate to think what's going to happen now when they know they can owe us a couple of thousand and we'll be lucky if we're able to get back a few bucks a week."

One certain effect of the new Garnishment Restriction Law, all credit card executives agree, will be a tightening of

the credit card distribution practices and eligibility requirements.

* * *

When the debtor isn't judgment-proof, and the burden
of debt becomes so overwhelming that it can wreck his life,
the law provides him with a means of wiping out his debt at
a discount. That's bankruptcy. The debtor's assets are turned
into cash, and the cash is used to pay off the creditors. But
if, say, all his assets convert into $100 and he owes $1,000,
he pays off the $1,000 with the $100. That's a 90 percent
discount. In other words, the credit card services get paid
off with 10¢ on the dollar. If they're lucky. Look at some
of the payoffs as reported in a recent issue of *The New York
Times* (the names have been changed and the payoff figures
have been added).

BANKRUPTCY PROCEEDINGS

William Olsten, machine knitter—liabilities $6,100; as-
sets $300 (payoff: 5¢ on the dollar).
Arthur Rosenthal, store manager—liabilities $7,867; as-
sets $225 (payoff: 3¢ on the dollar).
Paul Pearl, consultant and manager—liabilities $49,304;
assets $300 (payoff: 6/10¢ on the dollar).
Myra Riback, saleswoman—liabilities $17,154; assets
$80 (payoff: 1/10¢ on the dollar).

But even these payoff figures are high. When a person
goes into debt big enough to warrant bankruptcy, he doesn't
owe only the credit card companies: he owes other creditors,
and he's probably up to his ears in back taxes as well. The
taxes have to be paid first, and they come out of the assets,
before any of the cash is distributed to the other creditors.
When assets are as small as $80, $225 or $300, there's usually

nothing left. If there *is* anything left, the credit card services have to cut the pie with all the other creditors. Credit card services don't like personal bankruptcies. They won't ordinarily force a debtor into the bankruptcy courts; they usually have nothing to gain.

But *voluntary* bankruptcy is on the rise. One reason: Assets in the wife's name can't be touched. Another reason: Becoming bankrupt is almost a routine matter. The debtor pays a bankruptcy lawyer a fee of about $500 (it varies widely), and then finds himself in the hands of a "bankruptcy machine." That's a group of professionals who get up the legal papers, make the motions in court, notify the creditors, certify the books, put up the property for sale, collect the cash, settle the debts. The whole procedure takes only a few weeks, sometimes less. It's a psychologically painful experience, and the loss of respect in the community is something the debtor is not likely to forget, but mechanically, bankruptcy is a swift and simple procedure.

The debtor is wiped out by it, but so are his debts. He's no longer plagued with dunning letters, summonses, harassing phone calls—and the judgment no longer hangs over his head. That's the intent of the personal bankruptcy laws: To give the debtor a chance to start life anew. When the laws were written, the whole notion of personal debt was so morally unacceptable that the legislators were certain that personal bankruptcy laws would be invoked voluntarily only in the exceptional hardship case. They couldn't have forseen the credit card and debt as a way of life. While few card holders pile up debts with the idea of bankruptcy in mind (that's fraud, and it's punished by stiff fines and jail sentences) perhaps in the back of many card holders' minds is the feeling that if things ever do go sour, the bankruptcy courts could sweeten it up. Last year, the courts did just that—for almost 200,000 Americans.

Every time a debt to a credit card service is unpaid, it's eventually paid—by *you*. This has been a recurring theme in this book, but we repeat it once more, because of its vital importance: Whenever a credit card service is "taken," it takes out its losses on you. The credit card services puts the bite on the retailer, the retailer takes a bite out of your pocketbook in turn, and that's the start of a chain reaction which explodes into the mushrooming prices that burn up your salary check and your savings. Unpaid credit card debts lead to what Professor Mishan, of the London School of Economics, calls an "illfare" society because the welfare of everybody, whether they use credit cards or not, is turned into illfare. Unmanageable credit card debt and the illfare that inevitably festers from it, must be fought with vigor and without let-up.

How can *you* avoid unmanageable credit card debt? Chances are you don't have any problem doing it at all. There are some who never get into unmanageable debt even though they make hundreds of credit transactions a year—and you may be one of those people. On the other hand, there are hundreds of thousands of Americans to whom debts are, according to a spokesman for the Continental Illinois Bank of Chicago, "a constant and crushing burden." These are the *debt-prone,* and if you are one of *them,* you could be in danger. *Are* you one of them? Here's how to tell:

TO FIND OUT WHETHER *YOU* ARE DEBT-PRONE, MAKE THIS TEST

Are you an impulsive buyer?
☑ YES   ☐ NO

Do you go on buying sprees to get rid of the blues?
☐ YES   ☑ NO

Do you buy things with your credit card that you never

would buy with cash?

□ YES   ☑ NO

Do you tend to pick up the check when you can "charge it"?

□ YES   ☐ NO

Do you charge now and hope to pay for it with the raise in pay you expect later?

□ YES   ☑ NO

Do you spend your salary check without putting anything (or very little) away for a rainy day?

□ YES   ☑ NO

Are you unhappy with the amount of money you make and kid yourself that you're a big shot by charging luxuries you can do without?

□ YES   ☑ NO

Do you operate your household without a rigid budget?

□ YES   ☑ NO

Do you give into your children when they scream for products pushed on TV?

□ YES   ☑ NO

When you buy with cash are you more price conscious than when you buy on credit?

□ YES   ☑ NO

Count up the number of yesses. If they're below 5, you're out of danger. If they're between 5 and 7, the warning flags are up. If you've scored between 7 and 9, you could be in stormy financial seas. If you've racked up all 10 yesses, the chances are you've gone overboard already.

Are there any preventive measures you can take to avoid going into debt—even if you *are* debt-prone? There are. First, go over the test questions again and steel yourself to say, "*No!*" to every one of them—and mean it. Then follow this:

FORMULA TO PREVENT UNMANAGEABLE CREDIT CARD DEBT

Make each of the following three calculations. Each will give a figure in dollars. Select the lowest of the three. That's your *monthly credit card safety figure:* The maximum amount of money your family can afford to charge each month without risk of getting into unmanageable credit card debt.

- Jot down your annual after-tax income. Take 20 percent of that. Example: Annual after-tax income is $10,000. Twenty percent of that is $2,000.

- Jot down your annual net income after taxes. Subtract the cost of your family's basic needs for a year—food, clothing, shelter. Take one-third of the remainder. Example: Annual net income after taxes, $10,000. Annual cost of basics, $6,500. The remainder after subtracting cost of basics from annual net income ($10,000 minus $6,500) is $3,500. One third of that is about $1,170.

- Jot down your annual net income after taxes. Multiply that by one and a half—that gives you your earnings for the next 18 months. Take 10 percent of that. Example: Annual net income, $10,000. Multiplied by one and a half, it becomes $15,000. Ten percent of that is $1,500.

You have now figured out your self-imposed annual credit card debt ceilings calculated by three different methods. Your ceilings come to: $2,000, $1,170, and $1,500. The lowest of these is $1,170. Divide that figure by 12 and you get your *monthly credit card safety figure*. In this case, for a family with a net income of $10,000, it's about $100. That's what you can charge each month without the risk of unmanageable credit card debt.

This formula is a result of studies made by banking specialists and economic experts. These men have developed these three methods for calculating self-imposed credit card ceilings. There is no unanimity of opinion about which is the best of these three methods, but the method that holds you to the least amount of expenditure is certainly the safest method. All three methods are based on bankruptcy figures which show that most American families in financial trouble have obligated themselves to pay more than 20 percent of their net income (the average is about 30 percent; many families have put themselves in hock up to 80 percent of their future earnings). Families who play their credit cards close to the vest seldom go over 15 percent. (In the example you've just read, the *monthly credit card safety figure* represents a little less than 12 percent of the net income.)

Suggestion: Use the three methods to calculate *your monthly credit card safety figure,* then compare it to what you're actually spending. You'll know at a glance if your debt is too much debt for you.

*   *   *

In its *Family Banker,* the Continental Illinois Bank cautions that as a "smart money manager, there's nothing at all wrong with using credit as an aid to managing your money—it's an accepted way of life. But you must be a manager in actual fact, and not let your debts manage you instead." The use of the *monthly credit card safety figure,* and a tight lip when it comes to saying "yes" to your natural inclination (if you have one) to overspend by overcharging, can help you manage. If you can do without the credit card, you should be able to manage even better.

Use the UNCREDIT CARD to get discounts. If you feel a bit shy about springing it on an unsuspecting store owner (you won't once you've tried it), join one of the consumer groups that arrange *in advance* with merchants to give you discounts *for cash* when you present *their* cards. In 1967, Dividends Clubs Incorporated introduced the "Money-Back Card" which pays the consumer quarterly dividends based on the amounts of purchases he makes in certain hotels, shops and restaurants. In New York, the Educated Consumer Corporation invites you to "10-20 percent discounts on every purchase, seven days a week at our fine participating stores and restaurants." One Los Angeles-based outfit is nationally franchising a "reverse credit card . . . a card that pays dividends if you use it instead of credit."

Repeat: Retailers on the whole are fed up with the high prices they have to pay to the credit card services (a Pittsburgh bookstore owner finds them " '. . . one of the most galling innovations in recent years,' " *The Wall Street Journal* reports. " 'They're a damn pain in the neck,' he gripes. 'The banks charge as much as 5, 6 percent and we do all the work— a damn lucrative thing for the banks!' ")—and most storekeepers welcome you warmly when you help them thumb their noses at the credit card services with *any* of your anti-credit card discount-for-cash cards. Caution, though: Group anti-credit cards can only be used in a limited number of outlets, and to use them you have to pay a yearly ($12 or more) fee. But you can use the UNCREDIT CARD freely—and for free.

It doesn't matter, though, what kind of anti-credit card you use. What matters is that you buy for cash—and get a discount for that cash. In that way, you're absolutely sure to escape unmanageable credit card debt—or any kind of con-summer credit debt for that matter—and you actually save money while you're doing it. It pays you to stay out of debt.

PART THREE

HIDDEN DANGERS IN YOUR PLASTICS: THEY COULD RUIN YOUR LIFE

CHAPTER VIII

Danger! These Credit Cards Are Booby Trapped

You can be stuck for thousands of dollars in credit card charges even though you don't hold a single credit card. That's just one of the dangers hidden in today's credit card system. Here's the inside story of how credit card small print makes you the victim of a new kind of crime wave, and the details of how credit card sharps can take you for everything you have—and you'll never know it until the bills arrive. Here, too, is how your reputation can be blackened, and your credit standing ruined forever, everywhere—even though you never defaulted on a debt in your life. An exposé of the credit card booby traps which will cost Americans hundreds of millions of dollars this year, and untold cost in personal anxiety and distress.

The start was as routine as coffee for breakfast. David Sanderson (his name and the other names in this story are fictitious, but the story is real) received a monthly credit card statement.

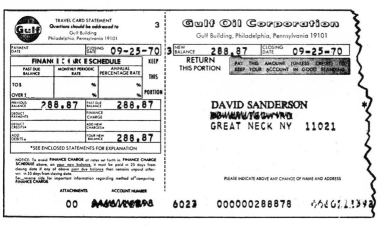

Only one thing was wrong with it. David Sanderson hadn't charged a cent on that card. It was a mistake, or . . . Sanderson quickly riffled through the cards in his wallet. Yes, his Gulf card was missing. He immediately notified the company of the loss in writing, and asked to see Xeroxes of his bills. They came. The bills were authentic, but the signatures were crude forgeries. The crook who had used his card had even misspelled his name. Sanderson refused to pay. Gulf, through its credit correspondent, R. F. Southleap, insisted on payment. Sanderson handed the matter over to his lawyer, Louis Forest, who wrote this letter to Gulf's Southleap:

LOUIS FOREST
Counsellor at Law
5~ Madison Avenue
New York, N. Y. 10017

July 3, 1970

Gulf Oil Company—U.S.	Att: R. F. Southleap
P. O. Box 8056	Credit Correspondent
Philadelphia, Pennsylvania	Re: David Sanderson
19101	9~ Arleigh Road
	Great Neck, New York
	Acct. No. 40~ ~~ ~9-8
	Bal. $288.87

Dear Mr. Southleap:

Please be advised that my client above named has asked me to communicate with you relative to your letter of June 5th concerning the above matter.

Firstly, will you please advise me as to the date on which Mr. Sanderson notified you of the loss of his credit card.

Secondly, in checking the purchase slips of Lou's Service

Station in relation to these fraudulent purchases, I note that Mr. Sanderson's "signature" is misspelled and that the serial numbers on the three (3) purchase cards are 8690058, 86-90064 and 8690067. It seems to me that in view of this misspelling and the close proximity in time of these purchases reflects quite a degree of negligence on the part of the service station and, under these circumstances, I am questioning whether Mr. Sanderson should be held liable.

I would like to dispose of this matter in amicable fashion and would appreciate some suggestion from you as to how we can do so on a practical level.

Yours very truly,
LOUIS FOREST

LF:jk
   cc: Mr. David Sanderson

Note the thrust of the lawyer's attack: It was the gas station that was negligent and therefore, his client, David Sanderson, was not responsible for the debts. Southleap answered:

	July 17, 1970
Louis Forest, Esq.	David Sanderson
ᵠᵠ Madison Avenue	ᵠ Arlogt Road
New York, New York 10017	Great Neck, New York
	ᵠᵠ 01ᵠ ᵠᵠ9-ᵠ
	BAL. $288.87

Dear Mr. Forest:

Thank you for your letter of July 3, 1970.

We were informed by Mr. Sanderson of the loss of his Travel

Card on September 24, 1969. This was accomplished by letter. As you can see, all purchases on Mr. Sanderson's account were made prior to that date. Therefore, we must request that Mr. Sanderson pay for these charges.

Also, since our dealer complied with our requirements of indicating the auto license number, and also cleared these purchases through our Telephone Authorization System, we do not feel that our dealer was negligent. It is not the policy of this corporation to require our dealers to check the exact way purchases are signed. If Mr. Sanderson would have reported his Travel Card lost prior to the fraudulent use of his account, when our dealer cleared them through our Telephone Authorization System, the purchases would not have been approved. Therefore, we feel that Mr. Sanderson was negligent in not notifying us immediately after the loss of his Travel Card.

If I can be of any further assistance to you, please do not hesitate to contact me.

> Sincerely yours,
> R. F. Southleap
> Credit Correspondent

The lawyer's thrust had been thrust aside. The gas station wasn't negligent, according to Gulf. It was Sanderson who was negligent for not having reported his loss sooner. Had Gulf's Southleap wished to hammer home his point, he could have referred Sanderson's lawyer to the small print on the back of Sanderson's credit card which we've underscored.

YOUR PASSPORT TO MOTORING PLEASURE

This credit card is the property of Gulf and is to be returned upon request. Acceptance by the party named on the front implies responsibility for all service and merchandise obtained hereby. Loss or theft hereof must be reported in writing immediately to avoid responsibility for unauthorized use.

BRITISH-AMERICAN   HOLIDAY INNS OF AMERICA   SKELLY

This credit card will be honored at Gulf stations and wherever any of these emblems are displayed in the United States, Canada and Puerto Rico.

GULF 7265H   **GULF OIL CORPORATION**

Who was responsible then, to Gulf for the $288.87 worth of merchandise—the gas station dealer who had accepted the forgeries, or David Sanderson, the innocent victim? To Sanderson's lawyer the answer was so clear-cut that he forwarded a copy of Gulf's letter to his client with the following cover letter, and closed the file.

New York, N.Y. 10017

LOUIS FOREST
Counsellor at Law

July 20, 1970

Mr. David Sanderson
Great Neck, N. Y.

Re: Gulf Oil—Bal. $288.87

Dear David:

Enclosed please find reply letter of the 17th to mine of the 3rd. It was worth a try, but not much more.

Under the circumstances he outlines (and under the Law

—I have checked some essentially similar cases) you have no choice but to pay, for failure to notify promptly renders you liable for fraudulent purchases made before receipt of notification of loss of credit card.*

You can send your check directly to Mr. Southleap, together with the copy of his letter which I am enclosing for facility of reference by him.

Cordially,
LOUIS FOREST

P. S. Remember what the horse said when it came in last—"You can't win them all."

L. F.

*   *   *

What happened to David Sanderson happened last year to hundreds of thousands of Americans. It could happen to you. You could lose a card by carelessness or theft and in just a few days be responsible for thousands of dollars of debt. Last year, according to *The Los Angeles Times,* missing credit cards cost people like you $50-million dollars. This year, the *Journal of Commerce* estimates, "bank card fraud [alone] is running at a $75-million-a-year clip . . ." Eugene Gold, Brooklyn's District Attorney, puts the cost of fraudulent charges racked up against the 1.5-million plastics he expects to be lost or stolen this year at $100-million, and that's a conservative projection. Credit card fraud has joined drug pushing, gambling, prostitution and loan-sharking in the nation's hierarchy of big-money crime.

The huge payoff has "attracted the beady attention of the Mafia," *Life* magazine reports, ". . . and brigades of thieves

---

**All underscores and italics in these documents are the author's.*

. . . [are] galloping through stores with [stolen credit cards] and running up disastrous sums in fraudulent . . . debt." The *Journal of Commerce* spells out one Mafia technique: "Small merchants . . . have been paying protection money to the mob for years. So when the enforcers come around to a small merchant with a sackful of cards and instructions to run $11,000 worth of bills through his printer [charge machine] in the next five days, the merchant has two choices. He can cooperate and keep half the take, or throw the bums out and lose his business to a firebomb."

Individual credit card pushers—"plastics pushers"—flourish, too. One of them confessed to *Scanlan's Monthly* that he "made his ample living passing . . . credit cards," and that he was "splitting for Japan . . . with a flat hundred grand in cash" after working the racket for little more than a year. He boasted that he had perfected his technique for using the cards to such a high level of safety that "they'll never be able to trace me, let alone catch me." He wasn't the only freelance plastics pusher, he told *Scanlan's*. There were thousands like him.

But whether the pusher is a loner or a syndicate hood, he needs cards with which to operate—and a new criminal sub-industry has sprung up to supply these cards. Going rate for a hot card is about $25 to $50, and that's high enough to entice the kind of criminal who has the opportunity and the cunning to steal the cards but not the guts or the savvy to push them. Chambermaids lift them from luggage, and cabin boys filch them from sunbathers' clothing and purses. Pickpockets now have a new reason to keep their fingers nimble. Waiters are not likely to return the cards you forget on their tables. When you're mugged or rolled, your assailant is as much after your credit cards as he is your other valuables. According to the F.B.I., purse snatching is the fastest rising crime in America. Reason: The crooks are after the credit cards in the purse. But the biggest source of hot cards, the *Journal of Commerce* has discovered, is your friendly neighborhood tavern where "some bartenders pick up as many as 5 or 10 cards a night."

Face it. Credit cards have spawned a new kind of crime wave. You're not safe anywhere.

*   *   *

You're not safe even if you never applied for a credit card, have no credit cards in your possession, and wouldn't have one even if they gave it to you. Credit card bills can still come to you, and when they come to you, you've got to pay them. Here's how it has happened to others, and how it can happen to you:

"Banks have found that the most effective way of starting a new credit card plan," Andrew F. Brimmer, a member of the Board of Governors of the Federal Reserve System testified before a Congressional subcommittee, "is to mail a large number of unsolicited cards. . . . During a single week this summer [1969] . . . more than 2,000,000 cards were mailed in New York City [alone]. . . ." In the four years, 1966-1969, about 100-million cards were "put on the air" (bankers' slang for "posted to consumers who hadn't requested them") throughout the nation. *About one million of those cards never got into the hands of the people for whom they were intended.*

Some of these cards were stolen before they reached the Post Office. Others were delivered to the wrong address or were snatched by mailbox thieves. And still others found their way into the pockets of "employees of the postal system," who, declares *Life* magazine, "reveal a fascinating capacity for dishonesty, [and] who steal [credit cards] from the mails and sell them for prices up to $50." Almost all these cards were used by plastics pushers to run up expenses of cataclysmic magnitude on the accounts of unsuspecting people in whose names the cards had been issued.

A 96-year-old woman, reports the financial columnist Sylvia Porter, received a bill from out of the blue for $1,600. She never even knew she had ever been issued a credit card. A 7-month-old infant (only one out of every five banks checked out their mailing list when they put their cards on the air, according to a survey conducted by a West Coast economic-legal team) was billed for $721.17—mostly in transatlantic fares. Throughout America, consumers found themselves victims of one of the strangest capers in history: They were being robbed of something they never knew they had, and they were being billed in the mail for the robbery—by a bank!

Remember: Even though they hadn't requested the cards, never even suspected they existed—the cards were in their names and, "Loss or theft hereof must be reported in writing immediately to avoid responsibility for unauthorized use." Generally, courts would not uphold claims against these charges, but in most cases, the cost of defending against the claim is more than the cost of paying. The unsuspecting "card holders" were stuck by the small print.

If what happened to hundreds of thousands of Americans hasn't happened to you yet, it still could. Only a few states have prevented banks from putting their cards on the air, even though Andrew F. Brimmer, speaking for the Federal Reserve System admits, "There are, of course, risks . . . opportunities for fraud . . . involved in the mailing of a large number of credit cards."

Moreover, you could be victimized in much the same way when you *apply* for a credit card, because even if you make

your application *in* a bank or *in* the offices of a credit card
company (and you don't ordinarily, most applications are
made by mail), your credit card comes to you *by mail*. Also,
whenever you renew, your credit card comes to you by mail.
Your card, in both these instances, could be stolen and used
anytime from the moment it's embossed with your name—
and you'd never know it. Until you get the bill.

*   *   *

But once the credit card gets into your hands, you can
really start to worry. If you're like most Americans and carry
a full load of cards around with you, it's like walking around
with a pocketful of blank checks with your signature on them.
An M.D., with a stack of cards 1¾ inches thick, dropped
more than $10,000 when his cards were stolen from the glove
compartment of his car. Numerous cases have been reported
where losses from stolen credit cards topped the $20,000
mark. One man lost $175,000. Actually, there's no limit to
what you can be clipped for when your cards are lifted.

Don't think that you can limit your potential losses by
holding just one card with a low credit ceiling. Daniel Orlich,
a Brooklyn exterminator, received bills on his stolen $400-
limit bank card for $1,636.02. Credit card ceilings can't be
policed, and the crooks know it.

Don't feel, either, that the new bank practice of laminating
a color polaroid of your head onto the back of your plastic
will make your card "so safe from improper use that it [will]
take a veritable Goldfinger to tamper with it," as Banker's
Trust claims. Crooks who couldn't make Goldfinger's third
team have long specialized in forging drivers' licenses and
passports—*Scanlan's Monthly* is the source of this survey of the
forged credit card underworld—and they find that switching photos on illustrated cards is child's play. Using your

head on credit cards will give you additional protection against the amateur plastics lifter, but it'll scarcely trouble the professional at all.

Don't, moreover, rely on your own vigilance to prevent your cards from being lifted. Of course, watch yourself at all times—but there are times, even when you're watching, that you can be taken. Ever hear of the "sleeve job"? It's a trick that's played in restaurants, on *you* at a time when you're at the peak of your vigilance: check time. Here's how the sleeve job is pulled:

You pay your check by plunking down your card on the check tray. The waiter picks it up, exits, then returns a few minutes later with your charge slip. You go over it like an auditor examing the books of a company suspected of a major swindle. You sign. The waiter rips off your copy, deposits the plastic on top of it in the tray, and departs. You pocket your receipt, and stuff the card back in your wallet. The card is safe and sound.

But when your credit card bill arrives, you find that the card which you believe is safe and sound in your wallet has been out running up hundreds, perhaps thousands, of dollars worth of charges against your account.

Your first reaction: It's another one of those computer mistakes. How could a card *in* your wallet be used by someone else? But *is* it *in* your wallet? You scramble into your pack of cards and, sure enough, there it is. But wait a minute! That name on the card—your name isn't Joe Greene. And that account number—you check your records—that's not your account number. The waiter must have given you somebody else's card by mistake.

Sure, he gave you somebody else's card; but *not* by mistake. He had that other person's card—and card lifters use a figure of speech taken from a crooked gambling ploy—"up his sleeve." That's the sleeve job: The switcheroo, one card for another. Very often the card that's switched to you is a card that has been reported missing, and can't be used with impunity. You're stuck with a marked card, the waiter walks away with a clean one, which he then sells. The switcheroo was easy, because as vigilant as you are, you're like most, you'd no more scrutinize your card when it's returned to you by a waiter than you'd examine your change to see if it's counterfeit. Had you tried to use that switched card without examining it, you could have ended up in a mess of trouble. You could have been accused of trying to pass a stolen card. Those innocents to whom this has happened know how difficult it would be to establish your innocence.

Usually, though, you discover the card isn't yours before you try to use it. But whenever you discover it, it's usually too late. And that's the point of the sleeve job: It gives the card lifters *time*. While the switched card was in your wallet, you didn't know *your* card was missing—and while you didn't know your card was missing, you didn't report your card as missing—and while you didn't report your card as missing, you were being robbed more thoroughly than if you had been held up at gun point. You'd seldom carry around in cash or jewelry the kind of money you could lose when you lose your credit card.

So don't be soothed by bank promotions that assure you that you won't be liable for debts incurred after loss or theft if you report the card missing within 24 hours of the loss or theft. The sleeve job is calculated to keep you from knowing that your card is missing for more than 24 hours. What's more, no sophisticated card lifter announces his crime. Skilled pickpockets have been known to lift a wallet, strip it of its credit cards, then return the wallet to the owner's pocket, without the victim ever suspecting he had been touched. Your own carelessness can go by just as unnoticed. By its very nature, losing a card, or leaving it on a counter, is an unconscious process. You're quite unaware the card is missing until the next time you want to use it. If you don't use your credit cards every day, that 24-hour safety zone some banks allow you is no better than 24 seconds.

If you do report your loss within the 24 hours, you may *still* be unprotected—because many shopkeepers team up with the crooks to *back*date your charges. You'll find yourself liable for charges made 48, 96, 192 hours before your card was lifted. And if you report your loss twenty-*five* hours after your credit card disappears, you can be certain to have no protection at all. In those twenty-five hours, one plastics pusher boasted, enough open-end airline tickets can be charged up on your account to take you around the world a dozen times. The crook sells the tickets at a discount for cash. But when the bill comes around, *you* have to pay it—in full.

Let your card slip out of your possession for even a day without reporting the loss, and you could be paying for months or years for what the crooks charged up to you. Only the credit card gives you this unprecedented opportunity for deferred payment: *Get robbed now. Pay later.* At interest rates up to 18 percent per year.

*   *   *

Worse: you're not even safe when your credit card is safely in your hands.

Ever notice the row of numbers in the upper right-hand corner of your service station invoice? Even if you have, chances are, according to the American Automobile Association, you wouldn't know what they mean. That's why you can be plucked, as thousands of motorists have, by still another kind of credit card crook, the service station gyp.

Those numbers—five figures, which can read anywhere from 00000 to 99999—represent the total cost of your purchase. If your bill is $3.75, the numbers should read 00375; if your bill is $17.20, the numbers should read 01720—and so forth. These numbers are imprinted by the gas station attendant with his charge machine. When the charge slip is submitted to the credit card service, it's those numbers that you'll be billed for. They should correspond with the amount of your purchase that the gas station attendant *writes* on your invoice. When you're being gypped, they don't.

The service station attendant, who may be the dealer, or a hired hand working hand-in-glove with the dealer, is taking advantage of your ignorance. He knows that the only number you'll check is the number he *writes* in. So the number he's imprinted—those numerals in the upper right-hand corner which are quite meaningless to you—are *higher* than those he writes in. It's the higher number that's paid the dealer by the credit card service—and the difference between the two numbers represent the gyp's illegal take. Of course, the credit card service won't pay him at all if the written numbers and the imprinted numbers don't correspond. The gyp *makes* them correspond, once you've signed the invoice and left the station, by doctoring his written figures. Three's are easily convertible to 8's—$3.75 can easily be made to correspond with 00875—and you don't have to be a professional forger to turn 1's and 7's into 9's. A split-second's penmanship makes $17.20 correspond to 09920. It requires little skill too, to drop a 2 before a $4.50 to make it correspond to a 02450.

It's a very successful swindle, according to the American Automobile Association's publication, *The New York Motorist,* which warns you to "Check Your Gasoline Credit Card

Purchases." If you don't keep a log of your expenses and compare it with your credit card bills, you're not likely to know you're being gypped. This author keeps a log, but only compared it with his credit card bills after heeding the AAA's warning—and he found he had been systematically gypped for 3 years, paying out 50 percent more than he should have. Multiply that take by the number of the gyp's customers—some stations service thousands—and you'll see that this credit card numbers game is far from small time. Two partners of a Brooklyn service station retired after 15 years of mulcting the public, each with more than a quarter of a million dollars in Swiss banks.

Used also by service station credit card gyps is the "extra charge slip" racket. When you hand over your credit card, the gas station attendant manages to slip out of sight—usually on the pretext of servicing another car—then prints up not one charge slip, but several. He fills them in at his leisure. And *you* pay—for merchandise and services you never bought.

Although this racket began in the service station industry, it has now spread throughout the commercial world. It can be used by anybody who can whisk your card out of sight without suspicion. A waiter, a storekeeper (under the counter is as much out of sight as into the back room), a salesperson working in cahoots with the boss, a motel owner or his cooperating room clerk. And as the racket has spread, it has gained in sophistication. Here's just one example of the kind of smartened-up money trap you can fall into when you hand over your credit card.

The retailer imprints the charge slip. The charge slip now has your credit service account number on it. Then—and remember, he's doing all this out of sight—he slips a piece of cardboard into the imprinter to prevent the store's account number from being printed. He uses your card to imprint your account number (and name, of course)—*on charge slips from other stores.* What has happened is that some local shops have combined to form criminal chain stores. The charge slips are filled out, the stores are paid by the credit card services, and the cooperating storekeepers or crooked employees, divvy up the loot. The bill comes to you—with back-up charge slips from stores you never entered or even heard of.

But that's no defense when it comes to not paying your bill. The small print on the back of your credit card always translates into one clear statement: While you hold the credit card, *you're* responsible for all debts incurred with it, no matter how incurred. You may think that since you can prove forgery was committed (anybody using the "extra charge slip" racket has to sign your name to the slips to validate them), you can get off the hook. You know that if your personal check is forged, and your bank pays the forger, the bank has to take the loss, not you. But with credit cards, the situation is topsy-turvy: In case of forgery, *you* have to take the loss, not the banks or the other credit card services. If they did have to take the loss, they would check your signature with care, as banks do on your checks, and this widespread forging of extra charge slips—a $10-million bamboozle—would be scotched. But the credit card services couldn't care less. Remember the heart of Gulf's response to David Sanderson? "It is not the policy of this corporation . . . to check the exact way purchases are signed." Your credit cards are not only blank checks on your account. They're blank checks that can be signed by anybody.

*   *   *

Use your credit card with the caution of a secret agent, protect it against theft, loss and fraudulent use, and you still may get a shock on your bill. This time, though, it's not the

crooks who hit you, it's the credit card services. Not fraudu-
lently, or even intentionally. But simply because they send
you information that you're not likely to read. Here's what
happens:

Because of the way bank credit card extended payment
plans have taken hold, other credit card services have added
their own extended payment plans to their bag of promotional
tricks. An oil company, a T&E service, or a department store
that never granted extended credit, suddenly does. They tell
you about it by mail in a series of announcements, at least
one of which contains a "disclosure sheet" as required by the
Federal Truth in Lending Law. But the announcements and
the disclosure sheet look like some more "junk-mail" promotion pieces, and you junk them unread. Had you read them,
you would have learned that if you don't pay your bill in two
months, interest up to 18 percent per year will be slapped
onto your unpaid balance. But you *do* learn about it the hard
way—when your bill arrives with the whopping markup on it.
    No use complaining. The way things stand now, you've
got to pay.

*   *   *

Take your credit card, put it in a vault, throw away the
key—and even then you're not safe. The computer's got your
number. And that can turn your life into an automated nightmare where, the nation's press reports, such things can happen as:

• Getting a bill for $371.12 from a credit card service
for a period when your credit card was under lock and key,
and being told by your lawyer that, since it would cost $500
in legal fees to fight the credit card company, it would be
cheaper to pay the $371.12. For goods you never bought,
never received, that existed only in the imagination of a crazy

computer. (Electronic engineers will tell you that when a computer's circuits are overloaded, it behaves very much like a human who collapses under stress: It goes berserk.)

• Fighting a more than $6,000 invoice on an unused, safely stored credit card, and watching your lawyers correspond with the computer for eight months before receiving an answer from the computer's lawyers. Then continuing to struggle for three years more before losing your case.

• Taking a virginal credit card, the only card you've ever had, out of the moth balls and attempting to use it, only to find you had been blackballed as a deadbeat because the computer claimed you owed the credit card service thousands.

• Receiving a flood of pay-up-or-else notices when you know you've bought nothing and nobody had the slightest chance of using your credit card. Finally giving in and sending the computer a check for the amount the giant electronic brain was threatening to sue you for—*exactly* $00.00—and getting a computerized "thank-you-for-your-payment-which-has-been-credited-to-your-account" note in return.

Whether you use your credit card or not, the computer can send you other people's statements, bill you over and over again for the same charges, multiply your interest rate dizzyingly, neglect to credit your account when you pay, forget to send you statements for months then threaten to sue, confuse you with somebody else and cut off your credit in 50 states, make your home-town merchants turn down any purchases you make except for cash—even though you've never defaulted on a payment in your life.

All these agonizing encounters with the computer have happened to some card holders, and will continue to happen to more. The computer has not been tamed. "No matter how sophisticated it is, it's still fallible," one credit card company spokesman admits. Another, responding to charges concerning the computer's muleheadedness when it comes to correcting mistakes, says shamefacedly, "The apparatus is so complicated that even the simplest goofs, like duplicate charges, take us months to track down." Critics of the computerized credit card industry suspect it's cheaper *not* to track them down. Particularly since you find it too frustrating to fight back (these days, the expression, "It's like talking to a stone wall," has been updated to, "It's like talking to a computer") —and in the long run, you break down and pay.

But you don't pay only in money. You pay in mental strain, in lost dignity and, sometimes when your credit rating is unjustifiably ruined, in a blackened reputation that can follow you wherever there's a credit card computer for the rest of your days. That's almost everywhere. The credit card can not only booby trap your money. It can booby trap your life.

CHAPTER IX

How To Protect Yourself
At All Times
Against Credit Card Booby Traps

How to outsmart the computer. How to avoid the dangers of unwanted cards. A basic list of DO's and DONT's for credit card safekeeping. How to get ready today, for the day you lose your cards. What to do when you discover your cards are missing. How to cut credit card losses due to theft and fraud. Here's a guide to de-fusing credit card booby traps, and learning how to live with your credit cards—safely.

YOU'VE GOT TO KEEP RECORDS. Don't think your transaction with a credit card service is finished once you've paid your bill. You could be billed again for the same purchase. And again. And again. It happened to a New York Congressman. The computer had made a mistake and he was dunned for more than $1,000 for merchandise that he had paid for two years before. But the Congressman could prove *that* he had paid, *when* he had paid, *how* he had paid, *what* charges he had paid for. He didn't have to pay again. *He* had kept records. But thousands of others, hit the same way, hadn't kept records. *They* had to pay again. Some of them again *and* again.

There's only one way to fight back against the computer's reign of error: Keep records. You've got to be able to prove in black and white that the computer's print-out is wrong. Do that, and there's no case against you.

Keep in a safe place, *all* bills, statements, demands for payment, and whatever other correspondence you have with your credit card services. Match up your canceled checks against the statements, and keep them, too. Keep carbon copies of *every* letter *you* write to the credit card services. If you decide to send your letters by registered mail return receipt requested (not a bad idea), staple the return receipt to your carbons.

Also, when you speak to anybody in the credit card service office by phone (or in person), get that person's full name, and be sure you spell it right. (You don't want them to come back later and say, "We never had any Miss Mohorovich in our employ," when in fact they did have a Miss Mohorovitz.) Jot down the name, the date, the time of the conversation, the reason for the conversation, and a summary of the conversation. Stash away that memorandum with the rest of your credit card keepsakes. It will come in handy when your lawyer begins to examine witnesses.

How long should you keep your credit card records? All states have statutes of limitations on debts, which means if, after a certain number of years, you haven't paid your debts, you don't have to pay them at all. In most states, it's six years. Check with your lawyer on the amount of time the credit card card services have to collect from you in your state. Then keep your records *that* long. They can't touch you after that, even if you *really* didn't pay.

Keeping records is not only your defense against computer plunder, but against all the other ways the computer can attack you. If the computer accuses you of being a deadbeat, your records can prove that you aren't. Your records can be used to fight other disputes with your credit card services not involving the computer. Suppose your credit card service denies that you gave them notice of a lost card—your records can help prove that you did. Once you write in your name on a plastic, you've *got* to keep records. And if it's a time and space consuming nuisance—well, that's just another hidden cost you have to pay for your credit cards.

*   *   *

HOW TO PROTECT YOURSELF AGAINST UN-WANTED CARDS. If a bank card comes to you in the mail, and you never asked for it, and you don't want it, here's what you do:

Cut the card in three or four parts. It'll take a pretty sharp scissor, but it can be done. Be sure you cut *through* the numbers. Never leave the number intact. Cut up in this way, the card just can't be put back together to look like new, and it can't be used in a charge machine—so you're safe against its misuse by anybody else. Then put the cut up card into an envelope and send it back to the issuer with a cover letter that says, in essence, *I don't want the card, take me off your list, and cease and desist from ever sending me a card unless I specifically request you to do so*. If you have a lawyer, send him a copy of your letter. If you have any kind of consumer protection set-up in town, also send a copy to its director. Let the local bank *and* the credit card service that franchises the bank know that you're sending out the copies. Chances are you'll never be bothered again.

What can you do, though, if you don't get the card, but you just get the bill? If your unwanted card is stolen and used *before* you know it's been issued to you, some states absolve you of any responsibility whatsoever. Others limit your responsibility to a minimal sum—$50, $100. So if you get a whopping bill on a card you never requested and don't have, call your lawyer first thing. You may be in a protected state.

If you're in an unprotected state (and that's most of the States of the Union), you're liable. But listen to Andrew F.

Brimmer express the views of the banking community before a Congressional sub-committee: "It seems evident that from a legal standpoint efforts to collect . . . from the intended recipient of a card for the unauthorized use of the card that is lost or stolen before it is received . . . would not be successful *even in States that have no statutory protection for consumers in such situations.*" So if you're in an unprotected state, and the banks try to collect for charges on cards you never asked for and never received, *threaten* to fight it in the courts. The *threat*—since, according to Brimmer, the banks think they can't win anyway—can cause them to get off your back. If you want to put more growl into your threat, write a letter, explaining the unjust squeeze the banks are putting on you, to your Senator, your Congressman, and all your City and State lawmakers—and send carbons to the presidents of the banks. You might even get apologies.

But if the threat doesn't work, consult your lawyer. He may agree with Brimmer that your chances of winning are good and take your case into court. One possible defense, applicable to *all* credit card liability suits is the small size in which the liability notice is printed (just see how difficult it is to read on your cards). When notices are printed in type too small for easy reading, courts have frequently ruled that the notices have no weight in law. So powerful is this line of defense thought to be, that it is advocated by several prominent attorneys. Remember, though, actual litigation may cost you more in lawyers' fees than you save; so weigh the costs before you actually get into the fight. If you do get into the fight, it'll be comforting to know that in some cases like yours, the scales of justice tipped *your* way.

*   *   *

HOW TO PLAY IT SAFE WITH THE CARDS YOU HAVE. A Dallas businessman requested a T&E card. It came to him in the mail. He used it at the rate of about $300 a month. Several months later, he received a bill for $7,217.17.

What had happened?

The crooks had filched the envelope en route, opened it, extracted the card. Then, with the connivance of several shady merchants, they printed up undated charge slips with the card. When that was done, they returned the card to the envelope and dropped the envelope back into the mail. Months later, the storekeepers put the charge slips through. The Dallas businessman was out $7,217.17.

So when a new card comes to you in the mail (and this goes for unrequested ones as well as requested ones) examine the envelope with care. If you have reason to suspect that it's been opened and resealed, advise the credit card service at once. Advise them also, to put your card on the hot list and issue you a new one. Follow this same procedure when your renewal card comes in the mail. If you see postal stampings and scribblings on the envelope indicating that the card had been misdirected and had gone to somebody else before it had been redirected to you, take no chances. (There may be disastrous charge slips in your future.) Insist on an immediate "kill" and a fresh account number.

Once the cards have arrived safely, treat them as if they were thousand dollar bills.

Here are some

BASIC *DO'S* AND *DON'T'S*
FOR CREDIT CARD SAFEKEEPING

Don't carry your credit cards loose. *Do* keep them in a see-through wallet. In this way, you know they're there all the time.

Don't leave your cards on desks, tabletops, in bureau drawers, or anyplace where access to them is easy. Children regard them as attractive playthings, and lose them. Tradesmen, maids, delivery boys, and even friends and relatives can find them irresistible. *Do* keep them out of sight and out of reach.

Don't keep your cards in your purse when you come home from shopping. Don't let your husband keep his wallet in his pants pocket when he goes to bed. *Do* secure your cards, when you're at home, in a locked drawer, strongbox or wall safe. That's no absolute protection against the professional burglar, but it's a help particularly if you're protected by an alarm system as well.

Don't carry all your cards with you when you go on a trip. *Do* carry only as few as necessary. Chances of loss on trips are higher than at home, and this precaution minimizes loss. Additional safeguard: When you're not using your cards, keep them in the hotel's safe.

Don't leave cards in your home when the entire family's away, no matter how confident you are of your security devices. *Do* deposit your cards in a bank safe deposit box.

Don't keep your cards in the glove compartment of your car, and never, never, never in your luggage. *Do* carry them on your person.

And

Don't carry an unnecessarily large number of cards. Even in those states where your liability is limited, it's not your *total* liability that's limited, but your liability on *each* card. If your liability is limited to $100 and you lose 20 cards, that could cost you $2,000. *Do* review the cards you now hold and see how many you can do without. The proper combination of four cards should enable you to charge anything that can be charged— and get up to two or three month's free credit (see Chapter II).

But with all the precautions in the world, the day may come when your credit cards may be lost or stolen. When it comes, you have to act lightning fast. And to do that you must prepare *right now*. Here's the set-up:

*   *   *

HOW TO GET READY TODAY FOR THE DAY YOU LOSE YOUR CARDS. This moment, take all your cards out of your wallet and put them on the table in front of you. Then, take a blank sheet of paper and write these headings across the top:

BRAND/NAMES/NUMBER/PHONE/ADDRESS/DATE

Pick up one of your cards. Under BRAND, jot down the name of the credit card service: Master Charge, American Express, R.H. Macy, Mobil Oil, etc. Under NAMES put down your name *and* the names of all other persons in your household who have copies of your card. Under NUMBER, put down the account number of your card. Under PHONE and ADDRESS, put down the telephone number to call and the address to write to in order to inform the credit card service of lost or stolen cards. You can get phone number and address from the credit card service's disclosure sheet. Or call the local issuer and ask for the phone number and address of the credit card service's "Lost Card Desk." Under DATE, put down the expiration date of your card. When you receive new cards, add them to your list.

You now have your *Credit Card Safety Record*. It contains all the necessary data you need to report lost or stolen cards. But it can also be useful to you in another way. Every few weeks, look up the expiration dates of your cards. As those dates draw near, be wary. You can expect renewal cards to arrive about three weeks prior to the expiration date. If they don't, go on record that you haven't received your renewal by writing to the credit service's Lost Card Desk. It's a safety measure that you shouldn't neglect. If your service is just tardy about sending out the card, no harm is done; but if your card has been issued and snatched in the mail, your letter could save you from having to fight against paying for a crook's charging binge. (When you do get your renewal card, destroy your expired one by cutting it into three pieces, as we've described. Then dispose of each piece on separate days in your garbage. If you have a garbage compactor, all the better.)

Important: Carry a copy of your Credit Card Safety Record with you at all times. Have all other members of your family using credit cards carry copies as well. Then, if you, or they, should lose the cards, you could act at once no matter where you are. The moment the credit card service receives proper notification of loss or theft, you no longer have any responsibility for charges made thereafter on your card.

* * *

WHAT TO DO WHEN YOU DISCOVER YOUR CREDIT CARDS ARE MISSING. The moment you discover your loss, get out your Credit Card Safety Record, and *call* the number listed on the line of the missing card. To the person answering at each Lost Card Desk, say, "I want to report a missing card." Give your name, address and the account number of your card. Make a note of the time of your call. Ask the name of the credit card service employee, and jot that down, too. Ask that a confirmation of your call be sent to you in writing. Ask that the time and date of the call be specified in that confirmation.

Your Credit Card Safety Record has just done you two good turns. It's given you the credit card Lost Card Desk phone number fast when you needed it fast. (Imagine trying to track down the numbers of your credit card service's Lost Card Desk when you don't even know in what cities they're located. Imagine trying to do it when you're abroad and you can't speak the language.) Also it's given you your account numbers. (Imagine trying to memorize, say, a dozen numbers like 250-031-246-597 and match each of them to the right card.) Knowing your account numbers may mean the difference in thousands of dollars to you. Unless you can give your account number to the Lost Card Desk, most credit card services hold that you have *not* given notice of your card's loss or theft. Reason: your card functions only through your card number (the card number activates your file in a computer), so the card *number* is, in reality, your card. Give the Lost Card Desk just your name and address, and it may take your credit card service *weeks* to locate your account number. All that time, you'll be responsible for the charges piling up on your account.

But once you've made your phone calls, you're not off the hook. We know of no credit card service that won't take immediate action to kill your card when you telephone, and won't regard your phoned notice as establishing the date and time of notification. But your phone call must be confirmed *in writing*.

Watch out: There are many kinds of "written notice" requirements, and they can spell trouble. Here are some, and here's how to meet them.

Almost all credit card services will accept telegrams or cables as written notification. Send them with the same information that you gave the Lost Card Desk on the phone. You'll find the addresses on your Credit Card Safety Record, and that's a third way the record comes to your rescue. Warning: cables are faster than airmail if you're abroad, but telegrams may not be if you're at home. Moreover, most telegrams are currently "delivered" by phone, with a mailed confirmation. That's just what you don't want. You want speed because your phoned notice is not technically valid until the credit card service *receives* your *written* notice, and you never know when you'll be hung up on a technicality. So if you're using telegrams, specify "hand delivery." It's also not a bad idea if you make the same specification when you cable. Always ask for copies of your cables or telegrams. Remember: you've *got* to keep records.

Some credit card services insist that written notice be made by registered mail. You'll have to comply. If your loss occurs at night or during weekends or holidays, you'll lose time until the Post Office opens, but there's nothing that can be done. Get to the Post Office as fast as possible and send off your registered letters (they contain the same information as the telegrams or cables) by the fastest possible way. Send them return receipt requested. Keep carbons of your letters and staple the returned receipts to them. Some credit card services will accept regular first class mail; but even if it's acceptable to them, it may not be preferable for you. It's always safer to have a return receipt of a registered letter in your files—just in case.

Other credit card services insist that you make your report *in person,* then sign a written statement. This is something like giving a legal deposition. Again, you'll have to comply —even if it means canceling a holiday and flying back home.

To meet the demands of some credit card services, you must have your signature on your written statements notarized. Many services thrust forms at you which you must fill out *in addition* to your written notification. A recent survey showed that it takes ten telegrams, twelve letters (three of which must be notarized) and eight special forms to provide proper notification for the loss or theft of credit cards contained in an average wallet.

What constitutes "written notice" can vary from credit card service to credit card service. Moreover, the requirements of each service are in a state of flux; what was required yesterday may not be what will be required tomorrow. Disclosure sheets do *not* spell out what written notice means in precise terms. What you have to do, to play it safe, is request a statement from the Lost Card Desk *in writing* spelling out exactly how the credit card service wants a written notice to be presented. It's a source of wonder to us, in view of the more than 1.5 million lost cards expected to be reported this year, that the credit card services haven't invented a simple uniform form that anybody can easily use. But until such a form is invented, why don't you make one up for yourself? Something like:

BRAND   ....

NAMES   ....

              ....

              ....

NUMBER...

The above card(s) were discovered missing

on....................at..................... and your Lost Card
        (date)   (time)

Desk was notified by phone on....................at
                                         (date)

....................by the undersigned who spoke with
    (time)

your ....

        (give name of person you spoke with)

                                 YOUR NAME
                                 YOUR ADDRESS
                               YOUR SIGNATURE

You can fill in the BRAND, NAMES, and NUMBER (get them from your Credit Card Safety Record) in advance, and address the envelopes to the credit card services in advance. You'll be that much ahead of the game on the day when you discover your credit cards are missing.

*   *   *

That's it. That's *all* you can do once your credit cards are gone. If you follow the guidelines we've just given you, you can do it as accurately and as rapidly as it can be done. *If* you do it yourself.

You can do it far more rapidly, and with a minimum of headaches, if you let a credit card protection service do it for you. One of the hidden costs of the credit card is the intolerable burden it puts on you to protect yourself at all times. The credit card protection service industry was founded in recent years to protect you, in some measure, from having to protect yourself. Credit card experts predict it could, in just a few years, boom into a multi-billion dollar industry.

Essentially, what the credit card protection services do, is make the phone calls and send out the written notifications for you. Here's how one service of this type describes its operation:

"We record your cards and card numbers at our Data Center. Then if they're lost or stolen you just call us *collect*. Twenty-four hours a day. From anywhere in the continental U.S. (From overseas you simply cable.)

"We'll immediately wire stop-payment notice to all your card companies. At no charge to you. Then we'll send you copies of those wires. So you have *time-dated* proof of the notification that ends your liability.

"Since you are liable for all charges made with your cards until you give proper (written) notification to the card issuing company, the important thing to do when your cards are missing is get notification to each card issuer *fast*. [We do it] for you electronically. Infinitely faster than you could do it yourself."

Most of these services supply you with a key ring inscribed with its hot-line number which is alive 24 hours a day. Some services permit you to call their hot-line phone collect from "anywhere in the world . . . Houston to Hong Kong." One firm gives you protection even in the event of a computer breakdown at its Data Center. It stores your credit card data on microfilm as well. These firms, charging $3 a year and up for their services, make credit card loss notification easier at modest costs. They relieve you of the tedium of some record-keeping, and they banish the anxiety associated with keeping those records safe. And, in the event you *haven't* prepared in advance for the day you lose your cards, they do it for you. Caught without a record of your cards, especially your card numbers, you could take weeks to make proper notification—while charges mount up dizzyingly. In that sense, the claim made by I. D. Registry, one of the leading credit card protection services, that it "can actually save you a fortune" is quite valid.

Two other major claims advanced by many of these protection services, however, should be scrutinized with care. Here's the build-up for one of those claims:

Main fear of many card holders is how to protect themselves between the time the cards disappear to the time the loss or theft is discovered. To allay that fear, credit card protection services have come up with a number of warning devices. A "hands off" sticker, for example, which you can affix to your credit cards WARNING thieves that your cards are protected by the service, so "hands off." Or a "thief WARNING membership card" which you slip in among your credit cards. The idea behind these gimmicks, according to a composite of protection service literature, is to "scare off a thief from using your credit card . . . by WARNING him that unauthorized use is dangerous . . . and that he has a good chance of being caught red-handed. . . . What does he do then? What can he do? Nothing, absolutely nothing. He drops your credit cards in the nearest sewer."

Here's the claim: The credit card protection service is "the one plan that can stop the credit card thief cold." And that *should* protect you from the moment you lose your card to the moment you discover it's missing.

Here's what the claim looks like close up: The professional plastics pusher knows that your cards won't even begin to get hot *until you discover they're missing—and usually that's long enough for him to score big.* Even in large type capital letters, the WARNINGS are not likely to slow down, let alone stop, today's sophisticated credit card hot-shots cold.

When a credit card protection service assures you that when you lose your cards, "Thanks to your membership with us, you haven't lost a penny. You'll be more secure knowing you're protected against loss," put *that* claim in the same category as "we stop the credit card thief cold."

If you discover your loss immediately (you're mugged, for example), and you call the credit card protection service hot-line, your liability, of course, stops at once. *Unless* your cards have been used to *pre*-date charge slips. The protection service doesn't protect you against *that*. Nor does it protect you in any way from losses incurred *before* you discover your cards are missing. The credit card protection service only protects you against loss if you use that service fast—*before* any debts have been charged up in your name; and it never protects you against pre-dated charge slips no matter how fast you move.

In short, credit card protection services are *protection* services only under limited conditions. Strictly speaking, they're *notification* services. Use them, with the full knowledge of their protective limitations, and they can do everything you can do on the day you discover your credit cards are missing—and do it a lot more efficiently.

* * *

HOW TO CUT YOUR LOSSES. We repeat: You usually don't discover your credit cards are missing until the plastics pusher has had a chance to push you to the wall. Face it: you're going to have losses. Here are three ways to cut them:

One. You can take out credit card insurance. Usually, it's a rider to your burglary policy. The cost is modest and it can protect you against major credit card losses. Coverage of about $2,500 should satisfy most needs, but go up to $5,000 if you want to be on the safe side. Actually, $5,000 could cover you for losses up to $15,000 or $20,000. Reason: Chances are, the insurance companies will fight any claim against you (they don't want to pay if they can avoid it), and their legal staff may settle a $15,000 or $20,000 claim for less than $5,000. It's happened—and you escape without having to pay a cent. Similarly, $2,500 insurance could protect you up to $10,000. Drawback: You usually have to assume a certain minimal loss before the insurance begins to be effective. It could be as much as $500. But even so, carrying credit cards without carrying credit card insurance is like living in a frame house without carrying fire insurance.

Two. You can become a member of a credit card protection service that *in addition* to its notification service provides you with credit card insurance. One service provides coverage of $1,000; another of $2,500. For charges above those ceilings, it's your loss.

Three. You can limit the credit cards you hold to those that are insured by the issuers. Chemical Bank of New York, for example, offers a Master Charge card on which your "maximum liability is only $25—even if you aren't able to notify the bank right away." (In addition, your unpaid balance is wiped out should you die prior to making payment— a boon to the beneficiaries of your estate.) With Chase Manhattan's Uni-Card, you're even better off. "Uni-Card," the card service boasts, "does not force innocent card holders to pay for the unauthorized use of lost or stolen cards." These bank cards *give* you free credit card insurance. Uni-Card's cuts your losses to nothing, on most fraudulent uses of your card.

Prediction: Because credit card services are fearful of restrictive legislation arising out of consumer demands for protection against credit card frauds, and because credit card services (particularly banks) are afraid that credit card fraud is stunting the growth of the credit card industry by making consumers too frightened to hold cards, more and more credit card services will offer *insured cards*. The day may not be far off when it won't be you who'll be taking the rap for the credit card crooks, but the insurance companies. You'll be out of it. Safe. And solvent.

*   *   *

You can protect yourself against credit card booby traps.

But those booby traps aren't the only dangers hidden in your plastics.

Explore now the terrifying world your plastics are shaping around you. . . .

PART FOUR

THE PLASTICS SOCIETY: IT CAN MOLD YOUR LIFE TODAY, AND TURN IT INTO A NIGHTMARE TOMORROW

CHAPTER X

Today's Credit Card:
Gift Wrapped Pandora's Box?

The credit card is packaged affluence. Since this credit need cost you nothing, it's packaged affluence wrapped as a gift. But take the gift wrapping off, and what do you find? An exploding social atom bomb, leaving a fallout of inflation, strikes, recession, crime, social decay, debt addiction, bankruptcy, and the potential loss of your savings. The credit card has more impact on your life today than any social innovation of the 20th century. For good or for evil? Here are the facts.

You're a member of an affluent society. Your income is 700 percent higher than it was for the same job in 1929. You've got a car, a home, a hi-fi, a color TV, a deep freeze. Your kids are slated for college, you vacation de luxe, you dress in style, you eat high on the hog. You own a washer and a dryer, a garbage disposal unit, a power mower, an electric can opener. You and more than 90-million other Americans will spend over $169 billion dollars this year on these good things of life. But you won't be able to buy one-fourth of it, despite your hypped-up pay—without credit.

What's more the credit needn't cost you a cent. Use your credit cards judiciously, and you can take two to three months to pay—without any charges whatsoever. The credit card looks like the greatest banking bargain of all time.

So there it is: the credit card, packaged affluence, virtually as a gift.

In Greek mythology, there was another gift like it. It was a box and it was given to a young woman named Pandora in the days before evil was known on earth. It was a gift from the Gods. It made her beautiful, wise, lovely, persuasive, talented, rich. The word "Pandora" means "gifted with everything." The box was her "everything card." She was warned, though: *Don't open the box. There's a mysterious danger hidden in it.* Curious, she lifted the lid. All the evils that inflict mankind exploded from the box like a mushrooming cloud and fell out all over the world. Is your credit card a gift wrapped Pandora's box? Let's take the wrappings off and lift the lid.

*   *   *

You know the root of credit card inflation: it's the hidden price you pay when the retailer passes the credit card service bite on to you. It's a stiff price. Add up service fees, membership fees, charge machine rentals, and all the other extra costs the credit card hangs on the retailer's shoulders, and it averages out to 6 percent of the selling price. That means for a month's free credit, you're paying 6 percent—or *72 percent a year*. The credit card is a banking bargain only when you keep the lid closed tight.

These higher prices are passed on to everyone, and the worker, trapped in an inflationary world he never made, tries to fight his way out with the strike. His position is understandable—he sees beans on the table instead of meat, no new spring dress for the wife this year. He simply needs more money to live on. But strikes are no longer bravura actions by heroic coal miners in some hill town a thousand miles away. The strike hits you and all of us. It has deprived us of the oil to heat our homes in mid-winter, cut us off from the transportation to take us to work, closed down hospitals, locked our children out of school for months, let the garbage rot in the streets. And when strikes end, and the wage increases have been granted—whopping ones now: 30, 40 percent or more to match the accelerating inflation—the increased wages are passed on to you in the form of increased prices. You suffer and you pay for it.

Business suffers, too. The rising costs of production—particularly skyrocketing labor costs—mean prices so high that many industries can no longer compete price-wise with foreign products manufactured by low cost labor. High quality, high fashion, but modestly priced Italian shoes, for example, have turned the shoe manufacturing towns of New England into disaster areas. Textiles from Australia, Southern Europe and the Orient have so undercut American prices that our entire textile industry, according to a spokesman, "stands on the verge of disaster." The American oil industry is locked in an international price war, and losing. Congressional lobbyists of the appliance, radio and TV manufacturers are consistently growing more urgent in their demands for tariff protection.

Hard hit, too, is the formerly impregnable automotive industry. Inflation had souped-up prices so much by the fall of 1970 that the small imported cars, assembled by German and Japanese workers earning little more than a quarter of the wages of their American opposite numbers, had captured one-seventh of the new car market. G.M.'s new minicar had been virtually driven out of that market because it had to be priced at least 10 percent higher than a Volkswagen. Inflationary wage rises, according to G.M. executives, have to be halted "if the American automotive industry is to survive."

This invasion of an inflationary American economy by low-cost merchandise from abroad (American businessmen, hurt by it, call it "dumping") is not without parallel in our history. It occurred just before the Great Crash of 1929, and culminated in the Smoot-Hawley bill of 1930, which raised tariffs steeply—and walled out foreign imports. Result of the Smoot-Hawley measure was to cut U.S. world trade sharply during the 30's and heighten the Depression. Inflationary conditions today, though, are much worse than in the years leading up to the Great Crash. To all the inflationary causes operating then, a new one has been added: the depredation of credit card inflation.

The credit card then, intensifies a special kind of industry-wide recession, which in the past has deepened into a general depression. It's a kind of recession too, for which past measures—like the Smoot-Hawley protective tariff—proved not only ineffective but actually worsened the condition, and for which no effective remedies have yet been invented. The credit card has helped put us in an economic box from which, at the moment, there is no exit.

*   *   *

Just as the credit card has spawned a new kind of inflation, so it has littered us with a new kind of crime. It's so new that Norman Jaspon, in his classic study of white collar crime published in the early '60's, doesn't mention credit card crime at all. There is no listing for it in the President's Commission on Law Enforcement and Administration of Justice's 1965 Report, and you can't find any reference to it in the Federal Bureau of Investigation's detailed summary of U.S. crime for 1968. It's only since then that credit card crime has grown big and tough enough to come under the scrutiny of law enforcement agencies.

But in the two years 1968-1970, credit card crime—plastics pushing and all the associated burglaries, robberies and frauds—has muscled its way into the big money. The take last year is usually set at about $100-million dollars, but that figure is on the conservative side. Reason for the low estimate: Credit card companies and banks are tightlipped about losses due to credit card crime since they fear publicity will slow down the flow of credit card applications. But in private, people who know credit cards will tell you that credit card crime cost American citizens close to $400-million last year, and this year might even double that. Prostitution, which has been around somewhat longer than the credit card, last year shook down Americans for only $225-million; and narcotics pushing, the most widely publicized crime in the history of American journalism, needled the public for only $300-million.

Reason for the sudden leap of credit card crime into the big time: Like the credit card itself, credit card crime is a mass production industry. Profits on individual cards are relatively small—from a low of $25 for the sale of a card to a take of several thousand for pushing it until it gets too hot to handle—and before a gross national total can reach into the high millions of dollars, multimillions of cards must be available for the plucking. Cards in these numbers began to be available in '68 as the banks' campaign to willy-nilly thrust 100-million free cards on the American public reached its climax.

As the number of credit cards in use continues to expand, you can expect an even greater explosion of credit card crime, particularly since the banks and credit card companies have come up with no credit card that can't be used criminally, and the law enforcement agencies have yet evolved no strategy for detecting and arresting the credit card criminal. Nor is today's feeble counterthrust against credit card crime likely to be helped by the tendency of credit card issuers to sweep the whole matter under the rug.

Which puts *you* in grave danger. For credit card crime has marked *you* as its victim. Just as each kind of crime demands a special kind of criminal (an arsonist is not likely to commit forgery, for example), each kind of crime demands a special kind of victim. You're not right for most crimes if you're an average American. You're going to have a beer tonight and not a fix; you can't be the victim of a dope ring. You're going home not to a brothel; no madam is going to overcharge or blackmail you. You're going to walk on the safe side not on the wild side; so you'll be out of the reach of street gangs and muggers. You work in an office or a factory not in a gambling joint; so the *cosa nostra* isn't going to strong-arm you into a rake-off. But as soon as your name is embossed on a plastic, you're a sitting duck for the credit card crook. And you can be taken when a bank sends you one of its free cards unrequested, even though you don't know you own a card. At *this* moment, *you* may be a victim of credit card crime.

*   *   *

Crime is not the only kind of social decay stimulated by the credit card. Follow this:

For the most part, what you buy with your credit cards are luxuries; you can live without them. But in a national economy that depends largely on your credit card dollars for its survival and growth, the production of these luxuries has become a necessity. There's nothing wrong with that. The sort of pleasant living that this kind of an economy creates is as American as the flag. But you can't buy a school with a credit card, or renew a slum, or modernize a hospital, or assemble a symphony orchestra, or develop an efficient machine for cleaning streets—so the manufacturing dollar just doesn't move in that direction. The manufacturing dollar goes where it gets the best return, to the credit card buyer, and our social and cultural services get shortchanged. The result is a curious mixture of affluence and decay. We sit in air-conditioned comfort and watch our polluted cities rot before our eyes—on color TV.

* * *

The decay is moral, too. The credit card has introduced a new kind of addiction: Debt addiction. One credit card expert states flatly, "The credit card is as addictive as heroin."

But as every dope pusher knows, you've got to take it in small doses first—and that's what "extended rotating credit" is all about. The doses are now so small that you can pay just about 4 percent of what you owe each month. That's almost nothing. You scarcely feel it. Just as soon as you've paid off one monthly fix, you go out and put yourself in hock for another. It doesn't take long before you're on the stuff for life. The stuff? Debt. The credit card pushes it to you.

Psychologists have not yet probed this strange compulsion to remain perpetually in debt—perhaps because it's so much a part of our lives that it doesn't seem strange at all. But one explanation: You live among people to whom incessant buying is the thing to do, so you do *their* thing. Another explanation: Often you're paying for things that you've used up, or can't be used anymore, or for which you no longer have any use; you've pledged your future income for yesterday's pleasures. So you go out and binge on new things to make yourself feel better—and start the cycle all over again.

A third explanation: Drug users go on the stuff to dream. Card users hold the stuff of dreams in their hands. For the credit card, in a pure literal sense, makes the American dream of the possession of a world of wonder products and services come true—continuously. The "plastic baubles in this promised land of Newfanglia [newfangled gimmicks]," insists Professor Edward J. Mishan, one of England's foremost economists, "outdo the greatest powers of hallucination." The credit card, like a drug, trips you into a dream world too fascinating ever to leave again.

But whatever the reason for it, debt addiction has hooked the nation. There are only about 60,000 heroin addicts in the U.S.A., according to the U.S. Department of Justice, but there are 81 million Americans on extended rotating credit. Or putting it another way: there are 81 million Americans who could be in hock for life.

*   *   *

As with most addictions, credit card cravings increase with continued use, and they have to be satisfied by larger doses of credit. This is fine with the banks who have been consistently raising their limits, and who invite you to stop in and talk it over if you want an even higher limit—with the odds heavily in your favor that you'll get it. Other restricted ceiling cards are following the banks' lead (they have to or be forced out of the credit card market), and on T&E cards, there are virtually no ceilings. There are few cards left—so powerful has been the competition of the bank cards—that do not offer some form of extended credit, and which have not raised their ceilings. With almost any card, you can go on buying and buying and buying—more than ever before. You can glut yourself by using more than one card. Few card holders carry less than six.

Expected result: overspending.

To help the family come up with the money for the monthly credit card fix, more and more women are entering the work force. These are women who, under non-credit card conditions, could afford *not* to work. "In fact," the U.S. Department of Labor's Women's Bureau points out, "the labor participation of wives is lowest (13 percent) in families with incomes of less than $2,000, and highest (53 percent) in families with incomes of $12,000 to $14,999. The middle income level reveals the largest proportion of working wives. The Labor Department statisticians add that nearly "half of all American women between the ages of 18 and 64 work." As late as 1964—the year before the bank card explosion—only one out of every five in that age group worked.

The sudden mass female invasion of the work force since then, due to credit card debt addiction (and to two other pressures to which the credit card has contributed forcefully: inflation and recession), has had a startling impact on the way we live. It ranges from disruption of traditional family eating patterns (a recent survey showed that only one out of every three families in which the mother worked took any of their meals together, due to the different hours at which the adults and the children left for and returned from home and school) to female demands for equal pay and working opportunities as men.

But even with husband and wife at work, as they are in more than 25 million American families, debt addiction overspending frequently becomes unmanageable. In the fall of 1970, one out of every five American families on extended rotating credit was finding it difficult to pay off installments and still have money left over for rent and food. One out of every ten families had fallen behind in their payments. In the newlywed group, the eighteen to twenty-four year olds who had bought their futures on credit, one in four families weren't paying when the payments came due. "Nowadays," a spokesman for Chicago's Continental Illinois Bank admits, "it's possible to go into debt much faster. . . . But sooner or later, the accounting comes, and the final result of debt [addiction] is bankruptcy."

Personal bankruptcy, rare only a decade ago, has now reached epidemic proportions, with as many as one out of every 25 families on extended rotating credit applying for this legal relief. This figure is even more alarming than it seems, consumer credit association spokesmen tell us, because it represents a sharply accelerating upward trend. If that trend continues, these experts predict, in just three years, one out of every four American families on extended rotating credit will be facing bankruptcy and, in the newlywed bracket, one out of every two.

*   *   *

Even though you're untouched by credit card addiction, even though you don't hold even a credit card, the credit card can be a threat to your savings. In the first six months of the Great Crash of 1929, 346 banks failed throughout the U.S.A., the *Federal Reserve Bulletin* reports, wiping out the lifetime savings of "untold millions." Result: Federal deposit insurance to protect you against bank crashes. Despite this Federal insurance, the odds are your savings can be wiped out in a bank crash—and the credit card is shortening those odds. Here's the scenario:

You're in a "recession pocket," a region of the country where the economy has collapsed. Like the shoe manufacturing towns of New England. Your income is down or it's out entirely, but you've got to pay the butcher, the grocer, the landlord, meet the rest of your bills and pay off your monthly credit card installments. You have to draw on your savings. Your neighbors are in the same sinking boat. They have to draw on their savings. Your bank is suddenly faced with a demand for large sums of money. It doesn't have it. Not because it's broke, but because most of its money is out working, in the form of loans—that's the bank's business. Only a small percent of the bank's assets (and this is true of any bank) is in readily available cash. And there just isn't enough of that cash to satisfy all the depositors who want to withdraw their funds. But you're not worried. You know your money is Federally insured—if the bank can't pay you, Uncle Sam will. How fast? You'll have your money in a few days, or a couple of weeks, at the most. True, if your money is in a checking account. But now for a shocker: *not true* if your money is in a savings account.

That's the law. Banks must pay up on checking account ("demand" deposits) on demand, and if they can't, the Federal insurance agency steps in and makes the payments for them. But when banks can't pay off on savings account deposits, they're legally required to declare a "payment moratorium" (a waiting period) before you, or any of its savings account depositors, can be paid off. Duration of that waiting period starts at 30 days and can extend as long as 9 months. And that goes for Savings and Loan Associations (S & L's), a special kind of bank-like financial institution.

Tough on you, but the legislators had a sound reason for writing the moratorium into the law. It gives the banks time to turn their assets into cash—and that should save your deposits, and save the banks as well. Here's why: Without the time out, the banks would not have been able to meet the withdrawal demands—and that's a definition of bank failure. The banks would have to go out of business. The payment moratorium was designed as a safeguard against bank failure. So for the good of the banking system and for the good of the economy—because the banking system depends on the economy—and therefore, for your long-range good, you have to sacrifice your money for up to nine months; at a time when you need it yesterday. Despite your hardship, the law makes social sense if it does achieve its aims—but does it?

Isn't it likely that once the bank declares a moratorium, you'll lose faith in the bank—particularly since you're in a recession pocket and you see businesses crumbling all around you? Isn't it likely that you'll immediately request the withdrawal of *all* your savings effective the first available date? And isn't it likely that all your neighbors will do the same?

It's more than likely. It's almost certain. So what began as a moderately high demand on savings deposit funds, now becomes a run on the bank. And a run on the bank always closes a bank down—for good. The payment moratorium, far from being a safeguard *against* failure, may be a guarantee *of* failure.

And failure, not only for your bank—but for other banks (and S & L's) as well. The history of mass bank failures demonstrates that a run on the bank is a contagious fever. It spreads rapidly into an epidemic, particularly in the morbid atmosphere of a recession. Every bank in your recession pocket will be hit by it. And already weakened by the general economic conditions, the chances are that one after another, they'll fall. Your bank was the first to topple in a row of dominos. You're caught now in a mass bank failure; but you have hope. You know that once *your* bank *has* failed, *then* you *can* collect your "Federally insured" savings from the government. But at times like this, with insurance claims being made on many banks at once, the brutal fact is: The government insuring agency may not have enough money to pay you.

Explanation:

Your bank accounts are not federally insured.

They're Federal agency insured.

And that's a big difference. The difference between getting paid or not.

If your bank accounts were federally insured, the virtually unlimited funds of the nation would stand behind them. But only the funds of the two federal agencies—the Federal Deposit Insurance Corporation (FDIC), and the Federal

Savings and Loan Insurance Corporation (FSLIC)—back them up, and these funds are limited. To pay off deposit insurance claims, these Federal agencies can raise cash from three sources: from their own assets, from what they can borrow under the law from the U. S. Treasury, and from the sale of the assets of the failed banks. Combining their own assets and the totals of what they're allowed to borrow from the Treasury, the FDIC and the FSLIC can jointly only ante up about $10 billion. But there are over $1,000 billion on deposit—all fully insured. That means: if the agencies had to make good only *one* percent of the nation's "Federally insured" deposits, it would leave them with a balance of zero dollars. If, at this time depositors were still unpaid, and it may take no more than the failure of eight banks during a short period to bring about this situation according to a warning sounded by the Comptroller General in 1964, then the Federal insurance agencies would have to depend on their third source of funds: the seized assets of the banks that have failed.

These assets are mostly loans, and the agencies would offer them for sale (to the remaining banks and other financial institutions) for as much money as they could get, as rapidly as they could get it. When the loans are "hard paper"—that is to say, when they're soundly secured by collateral—the agencies can easily dispose of them, and enough money can be raised to meet the depositors' demands. But when a sizeable portion of the loans are "soft paper"—unsecured loans— the agencies won't be able to find buyers for them anywhere, particularly in time of recession. There just wouldn't be enough money to meet the depositors' demands.

Today, a sizeable portion of bank loans *is* "soft paper."

Credit card loans.

The only security the credit card holder provides is his ability to earn money *in the future*. When the agencies are hard-pressed for cash, they need the money *now*. They can't get it from the credit card holders, nor can they get it from selling the loans. Who would buy paper secured by job futures which, in recession pockets, no longer exist?

So the Federal insurance agencies can no longer rely on the seized assets of failed banks to save your deposits should a sizeable number of bank failures occur at about the same time. This could occur at any time in the several pockets of recession that spot the country. If you live in any of these areas, the credit card has placed your savings in jeopardy. Remember: If the banks of any area topple and some depositors are not paid off, it could start a panic that could spread to the rest of this economically insecure nation. If you live any place in the U.S.A., the credit card is a threat to your savings.

*   *   *

The credit card, by bringing the benefits of consumer credit to the great masses of the people, has helped to give us today's democracy of affluence; but it has also given us a new kind of inflation, a new kind of crime and a new kind of addiction. It has contributed to the decay of our social and cultural institutions, and has had disturbing effects on the patterns of our everyday life. It is thrusting millions of families to the cliff-edge of bankruptcy, and it's a potential danger to the security of our savings.

Gift wrapped Pandora's box?

Yes.

CHAPTER XI

Tomorrow's Credit Card— It Will Buy Everything Except Freedom

---

The credit card and the computer are bringing you to the verge of a world in which just one electronic card will replace cash, checks and all other credit cards. With it, you'll be able to buy anything you can afford. Without it, there isn't a thing you'll be able to buy—neither food, nor clothing, nor housing, nor medical care. They who control the card will therefore, control you. And that single electronic card is on the drawing board right now. Here's a glimpse into the terrible, freedomless world of the future, and the story of the "bankers' plot" that is seducing you into it.

You're a number. You have no privacy. You must conform or you'll starve. You're an ant in an automated anthill. You've lost your freedom, your individuality. You can't escape.

A nightmare? Of course. But it's a nightmare you might very well be charging into—with your credit card.

*   *   *

Follow the road to the nightmare.

It starts in the banks. With the check. And the bankers' desire to get rid of it.

They want to get rid of the check because it's expensive. To process one check—that is to say, to carry it through some 20 operations from its deposit to its return to the person who signed it—costs the banking industry about 12¢ on the average. But more than 20 billion checks will be processed this year, and the cost to the banking industry will exceed 2.4 *billion* dollars.

The bankers have a problem: They can't simply wave the check out of existence; it's too necessary to our economy. Nearly 80 percent of the nation's cash is stashed away in checking accounts. There are more than 79 million checking accounts in the U.S.A. About 90 percent of all payments are made by check. That all adds up to a massive machinery to keep cash flowing. Eliminate the check and the machinery stops. So does the economy. If the bankers are to get rid of the check, they'll have to replace it with something else that does exactly what the check does, but does it more cheaply.

What does the check do? It transfers money. Example: You pay your retailer by check. He deposits the check. The check is an authorization to the banking system. It directs the system to take money from your account and put it in the account of your retailer. That's money transfer. *Check* money transfer. To replace the check, bankers need another kind of money transfer. Modern technology is providing one for them: *Electronic* money transfer. It's in the development stage now, but when it's ready, it will work something like this:

Instead of paying by check, you present your money card. It's electronic. Your retailer slips it into a gadget. He talks into the gadget or presses a few buttons. Electrons whiz and whirl. The money is transferred from your account to his. In *seconds*.

Compare check money transfer with electronic money transfer. Check money transfer takes about 20 operations.

Electronic money transfer takes one. Check money transfer takes at least three days. You've just seen how fast electronic money transfer works. Check money transfer takes dozens of people. Electronic money transfer replaces most of these people with computers. Check money transfer takes acres of office space. Electronic money transfer takes up only the compact space of the computers. In short, electronic money transfer saves operations, time, personnel, space. It saves money.

How much money? the Federal Reserve Board wanted to know; and the Stanford Research Institute came up with the answer: *4.7¢ for each money transfer.* That's like saving almost a nickel on a check. And on 20 *billion* checks . . . the arithmetic made Dale E. Reistad flip. "We're talking one billion dollars in potential savings!"

Dale E. Reistad is Director of Automation of the American Bankers Association. He's in a position to speak for the entire banking industry when it comes to an evaluation of the cost research conducted by Stanford and other groups, in collaboration with America's bankers, to decide whether to stay with or dispose of checks. "Our experience has been," he sums up, "that the more research [we do], the more intense becomes [our] dedication to the need for, and the desirability of, a . . . 'checkless society' for our future."

Are *you* ready for a checkless society? If you're like most Americans, the whole notion of checklessness comes as a shock. You've always lived with the check. You know it's safer than cash. It's a built in receipt, a protection against being billed for something you've already paid for. It's a way of handling your monthly bills with ease and security. It's like the safety pin, you take it for granted—but you can't imagine living in a society without it.

Bankers know this. They know they've got to get you ready for a checkless society. They've got to change your

mental attitude. They don't need psychologists or public re-
lations experts to tell them how to brainwash you. All they
have to do is listen to the advice of the Federal Reserve
Board: "Before such a checkless system could begin to operate, the consumer has to become accustomed to substitute
some form of money card for the traditional [check]." In other
words, you have to be weaned away from the check slowly.
Before they put the electronic money card in your hand (and
save themselves a cool billion a year), bankers have to get
you used to the whole idea of a money card. They've got to
get you to use a money card, to become as familiar with it
as you are with the check. Then, when the electronic money
card arrives on the scene, you won't regard it as a shocking
upheaval in the way you do things, but simply as a *better* way
of doing what you did before. And what form should this
transitional money card take? Once again it's the Federal Reserve Board that supplies the answer:

"*Credit cards* [can] be used to prepare . . . for an automated payment system. [They're] a step toward . . . electronic
money transfer. . . . An interim and useful phase in the evolu-
tion of . . . the checkless society."

And that's the essential reason why banks have been rush-
ing into the credit card business in recent years.

*   *   *

Credit cards have been around for a long time. Some, like
department store and major oil company credit cards, date
back to the turn of the century. The T&E cards, like Diners
Club, Carte Blanche and American Express, leaped into popularity after World War II. Except for some halfhearted at-
tempts to cash in on the trend in the '50's, banks had shied
away from the credit cards. Up to the mid-60's that is. By

1965 however, the results of the first tests of direct electronic money transfer to bank computers had proved successful. The checkless society had become a practical goal for the near future and bankers, like Edward E. Bontems, then president of the United California Bank, began to see credit cards as the "first step toward the electronic transfer of values [not only for] over-the-counter store purchases [but also for] a wide range of services including rent, insurance premiums, taxes, mortgage payments, and the like. . . ." The boom in bank credit cards was on.

Ever since, the banks' strategy has been to get the cards into as many hands as possible. All of America has to be trained for the electronic money card of tomorrow. This accounts for the banks widespread and virtually indiscriminate distribution of unsolicited cards by mail. Between 1966 and 1970 banks issued more than 100 million credit cards to unsuspecting consumers. There was little screening of any kind. Some families received six or seven cards. Some cards were made out to infants and small children. The outraged cries of the multitudes who never asked for the cards, didn't want them and swore they'd never use them, created furors in our legislative assemblies. But the banks knew what they were doing. Give a man or a woman a free credit card and no matter how reluctant they are to use it at first, chances are, sooner or later, they'll dig it out of the drawer they buried it in (plastic cards are made tough to destroy—deliberately), and they'll use it, and use it, and use it, and use it. . . . Credit cards are addictive.

Result: Nearly 41 million active credit card holders in the two major bank credit card systems, BankAmericard and Master Charge alone, and a national total of bank credit card holders exceeding 61 million. Virtually all these card holders were recruited by the banks in just four years! What's more, the rate of recruitment continues at such a high level that by 1974, students of the credit card phenomenon predict, more than 79 million Americans will have become bank credit card carrying members of society. Then, as many Americans will have bank credit card accounts as will have checking accounts. It should be comparatively simple after that for the banks to eliminate the checking accounts, and replace them with the already existing credit card accounts.

*   *   *

But don't think that the banks are doing all this just to collect that billion dollar a year jackpot when the check becomes a museum piece like wampum or the two dollar bill. A funny thing happened to the banks on the way to the checkless society: They found they could make money. Not just money. Big money. Here's the story behind the killing:

With the number of customers willing to charge surging over 61 million, it was child's play for the banks to sign up retailers drooling for the business. In 1969, the number of outlets accepting BankAmericards leaped from 397,000 to 646,000. Today, outlets for the two major bank credit card systems total well in excess of a million. When you add the average 5 percent bite on the credit card sales of those outlets (BankAmericard sales, alone, topped $2 billion last year) to the 12 to 18 percent take from the consumers' "extended balance" (which currently runs about $1 billion, according to Federal Reserve economists), you'll see, as one bank card executive pointed out to *The Journal of Commerce*, that "the income goes straight through the roof." Once a bank has gotten over its credit card growing pains, 10 to 18 percent return on invested capital is a modest expectation. As a comparative yardstick, the money you invest in a bank when you deposit your cash in a conventional savings account brings you a feeble 5 percent.

With multi-millions in profits now and multi-billions in prospect for the future, bankers have no hesitation writing out the 10 figure checks necessary for the electronic hardware which makes all this possible. Without electronics, the bank credit card is unthinkable. Even the most efficient of the old-fashioned bookkeeping methods couldn't have made a dent in the mountains of paper involved in handling the hundreds of millions of credit transactions chalked up annually. Today, a computer—which is essentially an electronic superbrain—can capture the facts and figures of a sales slip in a twinkling of an eye, remember them forever, and feed them back to the credit investigator as fast as he asks for them. The computer in your local bank can handle 2 million accounts and carry out 250,000 transactions a second without blowing a fuse.

Most important though to the bankers is not the computer's capacity, nor its efficiency, but its technological potential. If it can handle credit card money transfer today, it can be developed to handle electronic money card transfer tomorrow. Said a spokesman for the Cleveland Trust Company, when, after holding out for years, the bank finally announced the issuance of a computerized BankAmericards in the Spring of 1970:

"... it's *technologically* the first step ... which will eventually lead to an automatic, electronic system for transfer of funds. ..."

The credit card, powered by the computer, has blasted you off to a jet start down the road to the checkless society. Remember that what the bankers hope to achieve at the end of the road is something quite simple. A more efficient, less expensive replacement for the check. An electronic money card. Innocent. Harmless. But the computer is changing the entire nature of that card. Watch the computer as it transforms today's bank credit card, like a scene in a Jekyll and Hyde movie, into the electronic money card that will buy your admission into the nightmare at the end of the road. . . .

*   *   *

It's the computer which gives the credit card its extraordinary financial flexibility. The bank card, for example, can be used to make payments in almost every possible way. Dale E. Reistad points out that there's a spectrum of payment methods. "On the one extreme . . . is the Total Payment Instantly (TPI): the customer owes the merchant nothing. . . . On the other extreme [is the] Total Payment Delayed (TPD): the customer continues to owe the merchant. . . . [In between] are all [other] existing types of payment systems, including . . . revolving charge plans, monthly charge accounts, installment loans, and I'm sure, at least 10 more specific systems that are now in use." Reistad adds: "The credit card . . . can be considered to range all the way [in the scope of its payment capability] to Total Payment Delayed (TPD)." With one exception. It's this:

The way the credit card system is now constituted, Total Payment Instantly (TPI) cannot be made, because the consumer isn't even billed for days or weeks after the purchase. If the credit card could be made to pay off instantly, it would become the electronic money card, which is the goal of modern banking. When that goal is achieved—and this is the important thing—the electronic money card will also be able to make payments in every way that the credit card is now making payments. With your Electronic Money Transfer (EMT) card, you will be able to pay any way you choose along the entire payment spectrum from TPI to TPD. Because of how the computer has developed the bank credit card, your new electronic money card—your TPI-TPD-EMT card—will not be just a substitute for the check, it will be your key to every kind of credit. Your TPI-TPD-EMT card will be your total banking card.

It will also be your total purchasing card. Today you can pay for almost anything you want with a credit card. *Almost* anything. Tomorrow, there'll be no exceptions. Today you can't buy an automobile or a house with a credit card, but computerized operations will shortly handle both these transactions. Automobile purchases, boasts Donald McBride, president of the BankAmericard service, will be the next great credit card "breakthrough." Many bank officials foresee little trouble linking mortgage and down payments to your banking accounts via your bank credit cards in the near future. Today, you can't pay your utilities, your hospital or your insurance companies by means of your credit card; but banks like the First National Bank of Arizona and the Denver United States National Bank, have taken transitional steps to remedy that. They've invented the computerized *Supercheck.*

The *Supercheck* (that's what the Arizona bank calls its version; the Denver bank calls its, *Super Draft*) replaces that one blank line where you write in the name of your creditor *(pay to the order of. . . .)* with 48 printed names of companies and institutions that you'd be likely to do business with. All you do when you use *Supercheck* is fill in the amount of money you want to pay each creditor listed, attach your bill stubs and send the *Supercheck* to the bank. The computer then simply transfers funds from your account to the accounts of your creditors. You've paid off *all* your purchases—and that could include purchases of gas, electricity, insurance— with just *one* check instead of dozens. From *Supercheck* to *Supercard* is just one short step. By the time the TPI-TPD-EMT card is perfected, you'll have gotten used to the idea of buying everything with just one card.

You'll also have gotten used to the idea of having your credit checked instantaneously the moment you do. That's an-

other advantage of the computer—instant recall of all the facts
about you that have an influence on whether or not you get
the credit, and a lightning fast *yes* or *no* based on those facts.
If you think these facts are limited to answers to: Do you pay
your bills on time? Have you ever had a judgment brought
against you? What's your salary? . . . and the rest of the usual
credit investigator's questions, you're in for a stomach-sinking
shock.

With the responsibility for decisions concerning every one
of your buying—*and* banking—commitments looming in the
computers' future, bankers are taking no chance that the electronic brain will jump to the wrong conclusions based on
insufficient data. Already, computer "memory banks" are stor-
ing up information on your school records, what you did in
the Army, who you married and when you were divorced,
where and how long you were employed and why you got
fired, who you do business with, how you stand with your
mortgage, and every litigation you were ever associated
with, even as a witness. An agent of a firm specializing in com-
piling credit dossiers told a Senate subcommittee investigat-
ing credit cards, that he was ferreting out the answers to such
questions as: Does the credit card applicant drink? Has he
ever been a member of a protest group? Does he associate
with radicals? Mostly, it's the deadbeats the bankers are on
the lookout for, so it's derogatory information that investigators try to dig up.

Another firm actually specializes in obtaining the kind of
information that'll blacklist a citizen from getting even a
nickel's worth of credit—and the firm has already blacklisted
nine million Americans.

If you think you can escape this prying into your private
affairs, take a look at these facts of life and try to keep your
knees from buckling: Atlanta's Retail Credit Co. now has

confidential files on 70 million Americans. TRW Credit Data, another investigative firm based on the West Coast, has already built up 40 million files and is adding to its inventory so fast, that in five years you could probably find every American who ever applied for credit listed there. The information is sometimes so private that the FBI is now buying 25,000 credit reports a year.

There are worse facts to come. You can now use your bank credit cards to pay for taxes in 10 States of the Union, and you don't have to have supernatural gifts to predict a rapid spread of the practice to the other 40. That means each state can draw on the credit information the spy-and-snoop firms are spewing into the bank credit card computers. Already 25 states exchange computerized tax data with the Internal Revenue Service (IRS). Private information is already beginning to funnel from the spy-and-snoop firms to the banks, then to the states, then to the IRS; from computer to computer to computer to computer. It's not inconceivable that in that final IRS computer will lie the private lives of every citizen, ready to be exposed at the flick of a button. Perhaps that's why Honeywell, Inc., has been awarded a government contract to develop a special type of magnetic tape for the computer that can almost instantaneously record, and print back just as rapidly, the equivalent of 12 typewritten pages on the habits, attitudes, and history of every person in the U.S.A.

Invasion of privacy. Consequent control of your credit— and what you can and cannot buy. Utter dependence on the card as your only means of buying anything. These are the ugly characteristics that the computer has already injected into the nature of the bank credit card. And these are the characteristics which will be carried over into the electronic money card—but amplified, magnified, accentuated. You can see why.

When the TPI-TPD-EMT card becomes a reality, your income will be entered directly by electronic impulses from a corporate TPI-TPD-EMT card onto your spool of magnetic tape in a central computer. Not income that you can dispose of as you please, but income that the computer has already disposed of for you. Because before anything is credited to your account, the electronic whiz machine will have cut out the chunks of your earnings earmarked for hospitalization, taxes, union dues, mortgage payments, gas, electric and telephone bills, bank loans, installment payments, clothing, groceries, cable TV, insurance, lawyers' and dentists' fees, baseball tickets, even alimony—and whisked them away to the magnetic spools of your creditors with the speed of light. You'll be paid through your TPI-TPD-EMT card account, and you'll pay from your TPI-TPD-EMT card account. Moreover, *what* you pay for and *how* you pay for it, will be determined by your card—because it's linked to the computer, and the computer knows everything about you. It knows what you can afford, and how you can afford to pay for it. Your card will tell *you* what's best for you. You'll be a prisoner of the card.

The computer will have turned the electronic money card —once conceived as simply another kind of check—into your entry card to the nightmare.

*   *   *

One hope: There may be rival cards. If there are rival cards, they'll be competing for your business. Why couldn't you shop around and use the card that'll give you—and it comes down to this—the most freedom? There may be say, a Bank America TPI-TPD-EMT card, and a Master Charge TPI-TPD-EMT card, and a Diners Club TPI-TPD-EMT card, and so on. *May* be. But the chances are against it.

Already, bank cards are driving all the other credit cards off the market. Reason: Computerized bookkeeping and mass sales brought about by the indiscriminate rain of free cards on the citizenry like manna from heaven, add up to big profits for the banks—while other types of credit card companies, lacking both mass giveaway policies and electronic automated data handling systems on a large scale, are finding it hard to publish an earnings statement showing earnings. Most T&E card companies are limping along. And one of the biggest of them has been lagging consistently in the red. It's likely that rival credit card systems will fold, or be swallowed up by bank systems—leaving tomorrow's TPI-TPD-EMT card solely in the hands of the banks.

Projecting the current situation, that means just two TPI-TPD-EMT cards will dominate the field, Bank America's and Master Charge's. That would mean two national electronic networks, each of mind-boggling complexity and costs that soar beyond our comprehension, and each duplicating the information of the other. This would represent waste on a scale unparalleled in the economic history of mankind; the megabillion dollar carbon copy. It is only reasonable to assume that the two major systems will come to some sort of accommodation with each other. A sharing of information and equipment, a partnership, a merger. Whatever arrangement they work out, one thing seems certain: There'll be one bank credit card system—and one card. Just *one* card. And one card will give you no choice. You'll use it because you have to, and you'll have to use it the way it tells you to.

One *last* hope: Cash. But that's like the U.S. cavalry galloping to the rescue on dead horses. Reason: You'll be paid *by card,* remember? You'll pay *with card,* remember? So what's the use of cash? Sure, if you had cash, you could plunk it down on the counter and tell them what to do with their TPI-TPD-EMT card. But in the world of tomorrow, it's *all* electronic money transfer, and that means not only no checks (mission accomplished) but no cash as well. Except perhaps, for small change to buy a newspaper or package of gum, your only money will be your TPI-TPD-EMT card.

It'll be money that can't be stolen or lost, because your thumb print will be embossed on it right over the electronic number corresponding with the number on your magnetic spool in the central computer. You'll have to impress your thumb on the embossing to activate the electronic connection. Nobody else could possibly use your card. "The bank credit card might become [not only] the individual's principle financial instrument," asserts the Federal Reserve Board, "[but also his] means of identification." To which BankAmericard's Donald McBride adds, "In this century, everyone will have an ID [Identification Card] that will be the prime medium of exchange." A numbered identification card for all citizens of the land of the free.

Since the bank computer circuits, which carry this number, will be linked to the Internal Revenue Service circuits, the government is bound to leap on your TPI-TPD-EMT card number as the official means of identifying you. Not only to the IRS because the IRS will be joined by computers to other bureaus. Already, Washington has begun the task of linking computers on every level of its bureaucracy, and, what's more, extending tentacle-like electronic cables into the states and the cities. Just one example: The National Crime Center has established two-way computer flow with 48 state security agencies and the police departments of almost every major city. By the time of the TPI-TPD-EMT card takeover, the government will have your number in every one of its departments. It will appear on your driver's license, your social security card, your Army dogtag, your parking ticket, your passport, your death certificate. For the baby born into the checkless society of tomorrow, the number will be tattooed on his wrist, stamped on his report card, inscribed on his diploma. . . . It will accompany him inseparably from cradle to grave. Your TPI-TPD-EMT card has not only imprisoned you, it's given you a number.

To turn a man into a number, as every prison warden knows, is to strip him of his dignity as a human being, his individuality, make it easier to get him to conform—because in a prison, "You do what you're told, and no talking back, see?" The number may very well serve the same purpose in the prison society your TPI-TPD-EMT card will usher in. And a prison society it will be. Consider the tremendous power to regulate our lives that the managers of the TPI-TPD-EMT computer complex will wield.

Today there's only one kind of business left that the consumer can influence, according to the eminent economist, John Kenneth Galbraith, and that's small business, retailing. Big business, he holds—big steel, big autos, big chemicals, big tobacco—the great corporate giants, decide what they want to sell you, at what price, then bring in the big pressure and persuasion boys from Madison Avenue to brainwash you into acceptance. Withholding your buck to try to halt this forced feeding of commodities is like attempting to hold back a hurricane with a fly swatter. But the little merchant, asserts Galbraith, is still responsive to the power of your dollar. Don't spend it, and he'll alter his price, his goods, his service to please you. Spend it, and you'll get more of what you want on a red carpet. But when the TPI-TPD-EMT card moves in, even this last vestige of your control will vanish. Reason: Your retailer will then be under the thumb of the banks.

Let the Federal Reserve Board begin to tell you why: "Retail stores . . . will no longer need credit and collection departments . . . [since] bookkeeping functions will be taken over by the banks. . . . [Banks] will also provide sales analyses, inventory control data, payroll and cash flow information." In short, the banks will become the retailers' financial manager, and it's the financial manager who ordinarily recommends the most profitable ways to operate a business. That includes what to sell, and what price to sell it at. But, unlike most financial managers, the banks will be able to make their recommendations stick. If your retailer doesn't take the banks' advice, they'll revoke his license to handle the TPI-TPD-EMT card. That'll be the same as putting him out of business. The banks will be able to place whatever merchandise they want on the shelves, and whatever price they want on the price tags. And you're going to take it. Because there's no place else you can go. You're going to eat, dress, furnish your home in the style of the future—bank style.

If you complain—well, you better not. Let the banks fail to honor your TPI-TPD-EMT card, and you won't be able to buy a thing. If you step out of line, you could have no place to live, no way to get new clothing, no access to medical or legal aid. You could literally starve to death. And what's more terrifying, *they* will know when you step out of line, because the spy and snoop industry, already big time in its infancy because it's so necessary for the realistic extension of credit via the credit card, will have grown to monumental proportions when there's no other medium of exchange except the credit card.

And "stepping out of line" means not conforming to whatever arbitrary standards of behavior *the banking industry* will set up for you. Yes, the banking industry. Not the church, the government, the schools, or even the mass media. With the power of life and death over you, there's no reason in the world why bankers couldn't dictate the conditions of your life until your death. About those conditions, you can be sure of this: The bankers want the society to run smoothly and profitably, like one big business—and they'll look on you, and all of us, as employees in that business. They're not going to hurt you, they're going to keep you well-fed, well-housed, well-clothed and contented, doing the work you're best qualified to do. But *they* will choose the food, the housing, the clothing, the kind of job you should have, the kind of contentment you should feel. Ants live like that.

Like the ant, you'll be a prisoner of society. You do what you're told, and you don't talk back, see? One difference: The ant was never an individual, it's his instincts that tell him what to do, his anthill is natural, he was born into it. But you're an individual. You can see your anthill being built —it's automated. You weren't born into it. But right now— and you don't have instinctual drive as an excuse—you're charging into it with your credit card.

Once in, don't think you can get out. The chances are the computer network will spread all over the globe. Already the biggest of the European credit card systems is talking of merging with the biggest of ours. Your TPI-TPD-EMT card will be your passport—from one prison to another. With your TPI-TPD-EMT card, there's only one destination: The nightmare world of the future.

That's the end of the road.

*   *   *

When will you get there?

In the '40's, the eminent British author and social critic, George Orwell, in his novel *1984*, predicted that in that year a shadowy organization, personified by a fictitious leader called Big Brother, would control the life of every man, woman, and child in the world. Today, corporations and gov-

ernments talk about their "image"—and that's what Big
Brother would be, personified "image;" the very essence of
a benevolent, but ruthless, brainwashing, freedom destroying,
totalitarian dictatorship. No one could deviate from the society because Big Brother, through an interlinked network
of electronic bugs and TV Peeping Toms, would always
be watching. Deviation would mean instant "liquidation," the
term used in the '40's by authoritarian regimes instead of,
and to soften the brutality of, "execution for failure to conform."

Orwell might very well have been writing about the
"checkless society," even including the shadowy organization
that will manage the world behind the façade of Big Brother.
For it's likely that the bankers who control the economy—
and "they who control the purse strings, control the power"
—will, therefore, be the real managers of the one card world,
but will seldom appear publicly. Bankers don't win popularity
contests. An "image" more acceptable to public tastes, perhaps a portrayal by a great actor-politician, may very well
be the Big Brother of your tomorrow. Three major distinc-
tions, though, between Orwell's fiction and tomorrow's reality.

To Orwell, the world of the future is the inevitable end
of the road of totalitarian oppression, both of the right and
the left; you'll be whipped, and coerced and brutalized into it.
Actually, you're being seduced into it with the sweet poison
of the credit card.

To Orwell, the intricately detailed workings of the automated society were plotted in advance by the leaders of the
governing political parties. The truth is that, while there appears to be a "bankers' plot" to do the same, there is, in the
sense of a conscious conspiracy, no plot at all. What the
bankers set out to do was simply to cut the high costs of
checking by eliminating the check. They no more planned

to pollute society than the automobile manufacturers planned to pollute the atmosphere. They had no idea of the nightmare that their move toward a checkless society would spawn.

To Orwell, that nightmare will envelop you in 1984. As a matter of fact, the likelihood is that it will come much sooner.

Currently—and this development will clue us to a more precise time estimate—IBM is engaged in a development program called *Operation OmniSwitch*. The prefix "omni" was chosen because it means (in Latin) "all." So what the electronic experts are working on is a computer switching system covering *all* the people, in *all* parts of the country.

OmniSwitch will connect centralized computers to existing telephone networks. Your retailer will trip the switch and activate the computers (one of which will hold *your* spool of magnetic tape) simply by breathing your account number into the mouthpiece. Immediately, the computer will respond in *spoken English* with a loud and clear recital of the state of your account. If you're O.K., the retailer will give the computer the details of the transaction, and within seconds, *his* account will be richer by the amount of the charge (less the kickback to the bank), and *your* account will be programmed to deduct from your balance on the due dates (plus 12 to 18 percent annual interest when required). From *Operation OmniSwitch*—the computer network for all the people —it's only one short trip down the road to *OmniCard*—the computer card for all the people.

The technology that will bring about the electronic nightmare world of the checkless society is available now, or is on the drawing board, or will be soon. To wrap up the development is simply a matter of putting all the engineering together. That this is the kind of thing that American technologists can do with unerring skill and dazzling speed is beyond dispute. It took only a few years, under similar engineering circumstances, to build the first atom bomb. And with what they've learned since about mass-engineering from nuclear and space projects, engineers can now move faster than ever.

1984?

Keep your eye on 1974.

Index

197

you make money
when you accept my

UNCREDIT CARD

instead of my
credit card   For details ➙

(For details on how to use your UNCREDIT CARD, please refer back to pages 69-74.)

- You have to pay 5 to 7 percent to the credit card service, right?
- So I'll pay **cash** instead of using my credit card if you'll split that 5 to 7 percent with me.
- Here's the deal: I won't use my credit card and pay cash instead—and you give me a 2½ to 3½ percent discount. You gain 2½ to 3½ percent and you have the money **now**. OK?